for Kristy, Hana, & Iris
. . . *careless on a granary floor* . . .

& for my parents

Table of Contents

Gray goose and gander,
Waft your wings together,
And carry the good king's daughter
Over the one-strand river
                    —Traditional

There was earth inside them, and
They dug.
                    —Paul Celan

Acknowledgements

American Letters & Commentary: "The Hut of Poetry"

Fairy Tale Review: "A Point That Flows"

The Kenyon Review: "Meditations in the Hut" (published in slightly longer form as "10 Meditations in the Hut of Poetry")

Literary Imagination: "The Indweller's Aversion" and "The Nightingale's Drought, the Nightingale's Draught"

New Orleans Review: "Typhonic Meditation"

The New York Times: "Puzzle and Music Box" (published as "Disassembling My Childhood")

Puerto del Sol: "On Verdant Themes"

Seneca Review: "The Laurel Crown"

Trickhouse: "The Song Inside the Bird Song"

Thank you to the editors of *The Best American Essays 2010* for naming "On Verdant Themes" as one of their notable essays of the year.

Thank you to Andrea Richesin for including "Puzzle and Music Box" in her anthology *What I Would Tell Her*.

I'd also like to thank those people whose patience, kindness, and advice made this book better than it could be without them. Thank you, Mai Wagner, Lou Robinson, Sergio Vucci, and Dan Stolar. Thank you, Leila Wilson and Suzanne Buffam. Thank you, Ruth Ann Quick; and thank you, R. C. Quick. Rebecca Beachy's art continues to be a needed company and guide. My colleagues at Colorado State University have been genuine supports in matters poetic, wonderful, and otherwise; keen thanks is due to Bruce Ronda, Michael Lundblad, Sasha Steensen, and Matthew Cooperman. Likewise, I owe Emily Cook deep gratitude for first introducing me to the fine folk at Milkweed Editions, whose care for books in general inspires, and whose care for this work is central; thank you, in particular, to Daniel Slager. I owe an unpayable debt to Sally Keith and Srikanth Reddy, whose generosity brightens these pages, and all those I've written. And brighter than all, the starriest star, thank you, Kristy.

Wonderful Investigations

Preface

Wonder, as a point of concern, denies its own consideration. It has the remarkable capacity to hide in the midst of its revelation. Wonder, to preserve itself, withdraws. It withdraws from the mind, from the willing mind, which would make of mystery a category.

I remember being told a story about an old culture that believed the center of the forest was holy and could not be entered into. Even in the heat of the hunt, should the chased beast enter into the sacred center, the hunter would stop and not pursue. I think often about that line—which is not a line in any definite sense, is no certain marking, but rather is itself somehow without definition, a hazy line, a faulty boundary—that marks the periphery. One side of the line is the daily world where we who have appetites must fill our mouths, we who have thoughts must fill our minds. The other side is within the world and beyond it, where appetite isn't to be sated, where desire is not to be fulfilled, and where thoughts refuse to lead to knowledge. I like the moment of failure that finds us on that line, abandoned of intent, caught in an experience of a different order, stalking the line between two different worlds and imperfectly taking part in both. Such a place risks blasphemy at the same time that it returns reverence to risk.

My hope is to approach such a line. This book begins in essays that in their perambulatory wandering seek to near those ways in which wonder, magic, ritual, and initiation continue to exert a numinous presence within the work of reading. But wonder denies the efficacy of such consideration—to think is only half the work. The other half is to cease thinking and to do.

This book's second half tells tales. There are four tales, each connected to a different age: child, preadolescent, young adult, and adult. The first story is most fully in the wondrous realm; the last is the least.

If there is a wish in this book, it is merely this: That through the whole, as per Plato's definition of a line, is a "point that flows," and that the reader may find that point and follow it as it flows toward that edge where the margin becomes a center, and the end of the book the hazy border to the wonder-world.

FOUR ESSAYS

The Hut of Poetry

The difficulty of being a nature poet is that nature always intervenes. The virtue of an honest ethic, to write only what one sees, to write only what one lives, becomes complicated by vision, becomes entangled by the experience of being in the world. Light travels over a course of time far more extensive than the miles it leaps across before it reaches our eyes. It takes thousands upon thousands of years for a photon to move through the labyrinth of the sun's dense center to the star's surface; it takes some eight minutes for light to speed from the star's surface to our eyes, where the objects it lands on enter our minds upside down, like bats sleeping in a cave. Light seems instant, but light is ancient; and if light is ancient, then so is the sight light engenders. To write what one sees proves difficult because sight is a medium whose breadth encompasses time greater than the limits of human consciousness. To see is to open one's eyes to a source that includes oneself. Light comes with a history that includes our own. To see is to see double: the self as the self seeing, the world as the world seen. We do this seeing over the course of the years by which we count the extent of our lives. Years add up to something, but they do not add up to the world, they do not add up to the self in the world. Who am I when I say "I"? Not a container, not a vessel, filling over the course of a life with the evidence of having lived it. Not a silo slowly filling with grain. Not a sufficiency. Not a gathering resource unto myself. The difficulty with wanting to write about the world, the nature poet's truest creed, is that one finds there is nothing other than the world about which to write. The world is a limit— but a limit whose boundary is evanescent, the drama of the horizon line. Definition doesn't enclose when it does its truest work; it enacts, or reenacts, a process already occurred, a process that never stopped occurring. It began as we began: a single cell, a singular idea, definitive, commensurable, and then a force moves through it and it expands through the limit by which it had been known, by which it had known itself. It moves outward. It breaks itself so it cannot stay known.

When I think about writing poetry now, I think about an exhibit of ancient southwestern pottery I went to see many years ago. I remember one bowl in particular: brown earthenware, no glaze, at the bottom of which, in yellow slip, an ant lion was painted. I thought the bowl contained a secret, that it lived a double life in the way poetry lives a double life. An object of use: the bowl was used to carry grain to feed the family of the man or woman who made it. An object of art, of mimicry: the bowl took its shape almost comically because from the sand bowl an ant lion joyfully digs, then waits patiently at the bottom for an ant to fall in and provide a meal. This bowl, in a sense, is a found form. The potter found her model in the ground at her feet, an aspect of attention all the more remarkable for the fact that the bowl is meant to carry food, and the ant lion's bowl-shaped trap serves the same purpose. Such work isn't imitation; it is realization through repetition, a form of conjuring, a form of charm, a "sympathetic magic," whose hope is that the manufactured object will share in the creative principle of the natural one. Many of the other vessels were broken at the bottom, the point where the burden of the grain or the water was greatest. Sometimes I imagine the work of writing as carrying that ant lion bowl in my arms, and as I walk, the grain spills out the bottom onto the road I'm walking on, so that each step buries the seeds back into the earth from which they were pulled.

The other image that comes to mind when I think about poetry is a spiritual object of the Bambara people in Mali called a *boli*. The *boli* figure in the museum I frequently visited had a vaguely bovine shape: four legs, a thick body rising up into a hump, and the hump slanting forward, as if in the process—as of a cloud—of expanding slowly into a head that had yet to fully form. The *boli* figure begins as a wooden block around which white cloth is wrapped. Then a mixture of mud, blood, and grain is packed in encrusting layers around the core, gradually building into the vaguely animal-like shape I stared at behind the glass case. The ambiguity of the shape keeps the object in almost constant refrain in my mind. The suggestion is of an animal that on closer scrutiny it could not be mistaken for—a work of representation in which recognition is triggered only to fail. The *boli* seems to find a shape that allows it to exist in the world I live in, this world in which to see it is to think of it as bovine in structure, and simultaneously another world in which such shapes come to no meaning, another world where every definite form dilates as clouds dilate when they distend and merge into the blue sky they had before obscured. The *boli*'s role in Bambara culture is to regulate the energy that moves from the universe into this world, as the atmosphere, and the clouds that fill it, regulates the sun's light. It is an object that keeps in balance a force, a spiritual energy, which unbalanced, could damage the world. Its likeness to a cow belongs to this world, this earth; its unlikeness to the cow belongs to the other world, the universe. It shares in both, and the oddity of its form is a result of the accuracy with which it performs its work. The *boli* is a form that attends to its own formlessness. It shows the body at the point of pivot between two kinds of existence. It shows the cost of belonging to two worlds simultaneously while being able to fully exist in neither. It is the object as threshold, a door which is open only by being closed. It is a symbol. Its life is a symbolic life and brings us who believe in its power to our own symbolic nature.

The *boli* is my poetic ideal; as is the ant lion bowl. I cannot differentiate how I think about them from how I think about poetry. They are of the world, of the environment, in the way I've come to believe poetry is of the world, of the environment. What unites all three artworks is their relationship to form. Poetry is an audacious experiment in form, with form as the means of the experiment. Language, paradoxically enough, often obstructs the more fundamental work a poem attempts to realize, filling the space of the poem with a worth that can be captured by the intelligence and removed. Such reading of poems for the value of what they may mean enforces a strict economy on poetry, a system of value that poetry itself is always trying to destabilize, to question if not destruct. But what is this work of poetry if it is not the work of making meaning through language? What can we find if we put our assumptions away, put our expectations away—if this can even be done—and turn to the poem for other reasons, other experiences? It helps, perhaps, to think of the poem not as content but cavern. It is not for us to ask, "What is it?" It is for us to enter.

Reading is a method of entering; entering is a form of initiation. Form seen as such means that the poem functions on the page as a location that ceases to be a location. The poem on the page is no principality. It does not make a distinct place *in* the world, nor does it make a distinct place *of* the world. It is not a site to travel to, not a place of destination. Rather, the poem denies location because it acts—as the *boli* figure acts—as a nexus between worlds, taking part in both worlds but belonging to neither, a threshold in which one must learn to uncomfortably dwell. The difficulty of reading poetry isn't the work of understanding what a poem may or may not mean. The truer difficulty is in learning to read so as to occupy the environment the poem opens, to suffer encounter with what is in the poem.

Our normal approach to reading, what we are taught to do in school, outlines a method whose end is a momentum that casts us out of the poem as the reward for having read it, our mind bejeweled with the profit of what we've found. To think of poetry as an environment, as a space of initiation, is to learn to read so as to lose a sense of meaning, to become bereft of what it is we thought we knew, to lose direction, to become bewildered. The first act of imagination in reading isn't the work of image making but the work of entering the poem in which images exist, inexplicable ornaments within the form, each promising a knowledge to acquire should one be patient enough to learn to see it. We enter the poem to threaten the security of the knowledge we possess before we read it. We enter the poem to be asked a question we will not ask ourselves otherwise, a question that begins at the point of our certainty. The fifteenth-century Indian poet Kabir knows the necessary difficulty of such work; he also knows the work's abundance:

Kabir says, seekers, listen:
Wherever you are
is the entry point.

When we enter as ourselves we enter as seekers, as initiates. The work of reading as an initiate to poetry is seldom a work that feels like reading. It is not active, but passive. It is learning to read so as to be read. Kabir, again:

A tree stands without root,
without flowers bears fruit;
no leaf, no branch . . .
Dance done without feet,
tune played without hands,
praises sung without tongue,
singer without shape or form—
the true teacher reveals.

Causality within the world the poem reveals is a faulty explanation of how tree, flower, dance, melody, and song come to be. The poem is the form the reader enters in order to see what the teacher reveals: that we dismiss the awful, inspiring fact of what exists when we attribute its existence to something other than itself. To the poetic initiate, the poem is the form one enters to hear the "praises sung without tongue," to hear the "singer without shape or form." Inside the poem the initiate finds the world turned around:

Turned-around Ganga dries up the ocean,
swallows the moon and sun . . .
Turned-around rabbit swallows a lion . . .

> Turned-around arrow strikes the hunter . . .
> Turned-around earth pierces the sky . . .

To describe the initiate's experience as paradoxical misnames its startling force. Within the poem each object becomes retranslated into its actual nature—each object becomes "turned-around." To be turned around isn't simply to appropriate the attributes of a contradicting object—river drying up ocean instead of feeding it, rabbit devouring lion, arrow hunting the hunter, earth stabbing sky. Kabir uses paradox paradoxically, contradiction contradictorily, to reveal, as a true teacher must, that the distance between subject and object is unsteady, is susceptible—within the world within the poem—of profound reversal. To read is also this work of being turned around. The turned-around poem reads the reader. Reading is a work done to us before it is a work we do.

But to better see what poetry as an initiatory environment might mean, we should look at examples of what such spaces are, of how they function, and what our own work of reading might be in such a context. Mircea Eliade, in *Rites and Symbols of Initiation,* outlines the nature of initiatory experience:

> The term initiation in the most general sense denotes a body of rites and oral teachings whose purpose is to produce a decisive alteration in . . . the person to be initiated. In philosophical terms, initiation is equivalent to a basic change in existential condition; the novice emerges from his ordeal endowed with a totally different being from that which he possessed before his initiation; he has become *another.* . . . Initiation introduces the

candidate into the human community and into the
world of spiritual and cultural values.

The ordeal of initiation occurs, as does a poem on a page, in a location
that is not a place. A sacred ground is prepared and on that ground,
or near it, an enclosure is built. The preparation of the ground returns
it to a chaos on which the enclosure as cosmos is built. The enclosure often represents the body of a divinity, and to enter it is to enter
the body, to walk in through the mouth, to be devoured. Initiation
requires death, to encounter death. In some cultures, initiates return
from the sacred ground to their mothers who can no longer see them,
mothers who wail in mourning at the death of their sons while their
sons, from the edge of the woods, watch them. Some initiates return
with a new name and no memory of their previous life. Other rituals
are even more startling:

> On a particular day the novices, led by a priest,
> proceed to the Nanda [a stone enclosure, often hun-
> dreds of feet long, a great distance from the village]
> in single file, with a club in one hand and a lance
> in the other. The old men await them in front of
> the walls, singing. The novices drop their weapons
> at the old man's feet, as symbols of gifts, and then
> withdraw to the cabins. On the fifth day, again led
> by the priests, they once more proceed to the sacred
> enclosure, but this time the old men are not await-
> ing them by the walls. They are then taken into
> the Nanda. There "lie a row of dead men, covered
> with blood, their bodies apparently cut open and
> their entrails protruding." The priest-guide walks

over the corpses and the terrified novices follow him to the other end of the enclosure, where the chief priest awaits them. "Suddenly he blurts out a great yell, whereupon the dead men start to their feet, and run down to the river to cleanse themselves from the blood and filth with which they are besmeared."

The link between such ancient initiatory ordeals and the work of reading poetry seems spurious unless it feels intuitive. A blank page is one version of chaos, and the lines built on that ground form a dwelling. It is a strange dwelling, meaningless before entered—a confusion of black marks on a white page. By reading it we enter it. Entering it we find a world inside it. Inside it we can see. We find ourselves in a world that does not exist by any normal measure of existence, a world we see within our minds that we enter only by attending to something outside of ourselves. The movement outward and the movement inward are simultaneous. When we read we hear the old ones singing. To learn to sing ourselves—that secret our initiation introduces us to—is to find ourselves walking upon the corpses of those who sang before us, pulling from their mouths the words we find in our own, giving to those words our own breath. When we learn to sing, the dead leap up and wash the grime from their bodies. Tradition promises us this resuscitating work. Such a vision of the poem realizes Emily Dickinson's aspiration for art as a house that "tries to be haunted." Dickinson, like Kabir (poets of deep congruence), provides help in other ways. Dickinson not only understands that the poem is a form that waits to be haunted, she also gives her readers a glimpse into what the effect of that haunting, what the poem as an introduction to death, might be:

I felt a Funeral, in my Brain,
And Mourners to and fro
Kept treading - treading - till it seemed
That Sense was breaking through -

And when they all were seated,
A Service, like a Drum -
Kept beating - beating - till I thought
My mind was going numb -

And then I heard them lift a Box
And creak across my Soul
With those same Boots of Lead, again,
Then Space - began to toll,

As all the Heavens were a Bell,
And Being, but an Ear,
And I, and Silence, some strange Race
Wrecked, solitary, here -

And then a Plank in Reason, broke,
And I dropped down, and down -
And hit a World, at every plunge,
And Finished knowing - then -

"I felt a Funeral, in my Brain" offers readers a lesson in poetry as initiatory experience. The poem's first line introduces us to death, but a
death that occurs in the mind before it occurs in the body. The poem
is that strange space we can only enter mentally, as the page refuses
the materiality of the body's trespass. But Dickinson, from the poem's
first line, subverts the assumption that thinking is a process opposed

to the body's materiality. Reading in this initiatory sense requires the mind to feel rather than to think; the brain becomes not the mind's housing, but that penetralium within which these mourners mourn, these unnamed people whose "Boots of Lead," with their heavy step, strike "Space" into tolling. The image of these mourners parallels how one might conceive of thinking—a procession of images, each a thought, that progress according to their innate logic through the mind's confines. The mourners here are thoughts given particular image, thoughts given an allegorical life. They seem to lament in their heavy steps not only who in the poem is dying, this self-same speaker referring to herself as "I," but lament, too, the funereal condition in which thought's trajectory to ideal knowledge has been irretrievably broken. Thought here does not think, it feels. These pacing mourners, these pacing thoughts, attend a funeral which buries an epistemology that easily links thinking to truth, and from knowing resurrects sense in the most nervous possibilities of the word. The brain tunes itself back to body an easier logic would repudiate. Doing so, it hears heaven not as Enlightenment clockwork, but as "a Bell" that only now "Being" can hear. That ringing bell marks death; it rings across the universe. The casket—like the *boli* figure—mediates, in Dickinson's poem, two worlds. One is the world where sense is but common sense. The other world is where Being is "but an Ear" and the Heavens "a Bell." Kabir's thought that the singer has no shape or form comes to astounding realization. For "heaven's bell" isn't a bell, and the knowledge its ringing brings—a knowledge not factual in nature, but rather, a resonating drone that vibrates within the being of Dickinson's Ear—results in the plummet that actual knowing is. Knowledge isn't reason, but the plank that, in reason, breaks. Song, too, sings via vibration. Every line of a poem is "a Plank in Reason." To "finish knowing" is to break through the floor reason has built. Kabir and Dickinson know the hut of poetry has no floor.

Dickinson's definition of how she knows when she's read a poem comes into a new light: "If I read a book [and] it makes my whole body so cold no fire can ever warm me I know that is poetry. If I feel physically as if the top of my head were taken off, I know that is poetry. These are the only ways I know it. Is there any other way?" The poem isn't funereal in its relation to death. The funeral occurs in the brain. As one vision of knowledge is plunging downward through reason, so a parallel vision of knowledge is the loss of the top of one's head. The image isn't meant to depict a decapitation. Rather, it depicts the removal of that other plank, the skull's top, whose plank is the basement of the universe. That plank removed opens the mind to the whole. It is a death that precedes life. To read is the most common form of encounter with the dead. The dead on the blank page need not remain dead. Time in the page is different than time in the world. The page is that impossible cavern in which no echo has ever ceased echoing, in which no word has ever died, though the mouths that sang them were lost in the earth centuries ago. Death in the poem is only a pause before rebirth. Death is but a delay inside the form.

Language offers a method of experiencing death without dying. Language in a poem builds a form on a blank page, and by building that form, brings into use the strange, chaotic power the blank page represents—the power of the unseen, unspoken, unsung world that could be seen, spoken, and sung. The poem on the blank page houses a creative center infinitely larger than itself, than its own lined confines, but a power that has no useful ends without suffering the impossible limit of the poem's form. The forging of limit through form is the poem's most fundamental work, and the result of that work is that the poem becomes not a vessel of knowledge conveyed, but a dwelling where knowledge occurs. What we find inside the poem—for those of us who learn to read so as to enter—is the language by which the poem is built. We find words and the world those words evoke. Words, as does the *boli* figure, live a double life. The semiotic crisis of modern poetics, the sense of a word's arbitrary connection to the object it names, the indefinite distance between signifier and signified that feels as if it threatens language's ability to name anything at all, is not a modern crisis. Language is the ancient crisis that introduces us, over and over again, to the necessary failure words bear in relation to the world. It is not necessarily a semiotic difficulty so much as it is a mimetic one. We tend to see poems as vehicles of semiotic information when the poem becomes nothing more to us than ink on a page, the flat plane of the second dimension.

When the poem becomes for us not a page but a structure, when it is a place of entry and so of initiation, when we are the initiates inside it, language's double life becomes of profound use. Regardless of the arbitrary relation of a name to the named, the work occurring within that relation, the work words teach us to do, functions just the same. We read and recognize the world to which the words refer. Words function magically in the poetic environment, in the hut of the poem. That words give to the world a set of names by which we remember, we know it is an accidental quality of the deeper work words do. That deeper work is a magical work. The words out of which the poem is built always attempt to enact the world they name, to share in the nameless fact of the world's actuality by repeating it, by replicating it, in the words by which it is known. Within the poem we find a world in addition to the world. We return to those poems that matter most to us not because we have something else to learn but because the world of that poem has become for us our home.

But a home is never the world—a home is a separation from the world. A poem is never the world—a poem is a separation from the world. The world we read, and in reading see, never stays a world. Language's gift to us is its failure. The enchantment of language is superseded in importance by its disenchantment. The pivot between those two extremes mimics death. We are given a world that we lose. A poem's formal life is filled with totems that deny the death the poem's larger work forces us toward. Lines evoke the process of ritual, an attention always broken before it's complete, where enjambment demands that the attention find a way to renew itself, to resurrect the image the blank margin has just destroyed.

Literary tropes mimic a magic that recognizes death, and in doing so, gives us the means to undo it. Rhyme, properly heard, refuses to let sound die, but recognizes that it cannot call back the object it records in its original state. Rhyme calls forward the same sound in new form, as if the deeper meaning of a word had little to do with its lexical content, and everything to do with the syllable chanting inside the definition. The body is different but the breath is the same. A poem initiates us into death so as to awaken us into life, into this world that requires new eyes to see. What unites initiatory experience throughout cultures is the necessity of dying so as to leave behind one mode of interacting with the world and enter into another one. My sense of what poetry offers us is precisely this initiation into death so as to emerge from the poem more alive. We ask art to give us new eyes—to do so we must learn to put our old eyes out. Light is ancient, and the mistake we most often make is in thinking that to see is an instantaneous work. When we see with new eyes we see anciently. Poetry offers us the initiation into such light, and through such light, a life that sees the world in the continuous present. We put time away when we walk out of the poem and into the world. When time catches up, when we become again all too mortal, we return to the poem in order to remember how to return to the world.

When we read as initiates, and when the space of the poem is the space of initiation, we undergo the ancient ritual of deserving to live in the world in which we're alive. We put "childish things away."

That state in which the world dangles likes a bauble on the string of the mobile the baby reaches her hand toward is replaced by entering into the world with the overwhelming sense of life's sacredness. Initiation is the introduction to the fragility of the world by which it is seen as most whole and holy. We see that fragility by recognizing our own—a realization that we must step through mortality in order to step past it. To read a poem in this sense is to commit a necessary suicide. No, that's the wrong sentiment, the wrong word. One might say instead that to read the poem is also—secretly, anciently—to prepare oneself sacrificially, to make of one's mind and one's heart that peculiar offering that lends life to the page being considered. In such a notion we hear Whitman's song:

> The smallest sprout shows there is really no death,
> And if ever there was it led forward life, and does not
>   wait at the end to arrest it,
> And ceas'd the moment life appear'd.
>
> All goes onward and outward, nothing collapses,
> And to die is different from what any one supposed, and
>   luckier.

Poetry initiates us into the possibility of just such a supposition, anathema as it is to any common common sense. We cease to be initiates when the world is real to us. Poetry is difficult because it returns us to reality. To get there we enter the world the poem opens within itself. We suffer the dizzying repetitions, the marvelous representations. We become the poets we read, come into this sense of ourselves only through the loss of the same. We are with Apollo in Keats's "Hyperion," waking to his own power:

                    —Thus the God,
   While his enkindled eyes, with level glance
   Beneath his white soft temples, steadfast kept
   Trembling with light upon Mnemosyne.
   Soon wild commotions shook him, and made flush
   All the immortal fairness of his limbs;
   Most like the struggle at the gate of death;
   Or liker still to one who should take leave
   Of pale immortal death, and with a pang
   As hot as death's is chill, with fierce convulse
   Die into life . . .

Life, world: we die into it. Words kill us. We lose the tops of our heads.
Then we open our eyes. Then we walk out of the poem into the world.

The Laurel Crown

I. APOLLO AS—

A god is simultaneous. There is no essence in the god that holds itself apart from his other qualities, a manifold condition mortal language cannot record, save by the awkwardness of the hyphen (prophet-poet-hunter) set in perpetual loop. But even that naming contains an order the god's own nature denies as accurate. Why can Apollo brag to Cupid about his hunting prowess?

> . . . I can strike wild beasts—I never miss.
> I can fell enemies; just recently
> I even hit—my shafts were infinite—
> that swollen serpent, Python, sprawled across
> whole acres with his pestilential paunch.

His arrow never misses because the arrows themselves are prophetic: they've struck dead their prey before they've ever been launched. They are a form of the god's own desire—a desire different from human desire. Human desire, as Socrates points out, arises in us from a sense of what we lack. We want only what we do not possess. But what does a god lack?

A god lacks only lack. The god's story, brought down into song, put to words the god himself need not use to express his tale, inflicts a peculiar damage on the god. It makes the god relatable, desirable and capable of desire. The poem itself provides by its lines a ladder the god unwittingly must climb down, and then the godly world and the human world imperfectly coincide.

For a god, for Apollo, desire accomplishes itself. It arises not from lack, but in the reconfirmation of his completeness. A god's desire proves him a god to himself, for what he wants is already at hand. The arrows are infinite because none ever need be fired. Like the god's own simultaneous nature, the arrows are in their quiver, the arrows are strung, the arrows sling through the air, and the arrows pierce into their prey all at once. And like their owner, they partake of his nature. The arrow in the quiver speaks prophecy. The arrow on the sprung string sings. The arrow in the hind is a hunter.

2. DAPHNE'S BEAUTY

Beauty is strangely singular: singular because it heightens the qualities of the type to which it belongs and from which it distinguishes itself; strange because within beauty is some unnamable quiddity, so that beauty is singular but no single thing, a quality everywhere but nowhere specific, which acts upon those who recognize it as a magnet acts on an iron filing. We are drawn to what we see but cannot explain. Beauty seems to speak, to call, to beckon us; it creates in us desire for which it also seems the source. When we walk toward beauty, when we pursue it, we do so because beauty seems to contain something of us within it, but a something transformed. We expect from beauty ourselves, but ourselves metamorphosed—an apotheosis of the self into god or into child, but a self only accomplished in the strangeness of that beautiful one who is not us. We must enter beauty; but beauty wants to stay inviolate.

Daphne's father, the river god Peneus, demands of her a husband so that he may have grandsons. He sees in his daughter the work at which her beauty hints—that work of drawing forth whose consequence is generation. But Daphne wants none of it:

> . . . But his daughter scorns,
> as things quite criminal, the marriage torch
> and matrimony; with a modest blush
> on her fair face, she twines her arms around
> her father's neck: "Allow me to enjoy
> perpetual virginity," she pleads;
> "o dear, dear father, surely you'll concede
> to me the gift Diana has received
> from her dear father."

Beauty does its own knowing within the beautiful, almost a separate life within Daphne's life—and so she blushes in recognition of the erotic while at the same time she pleads to be saved from it. Beauty expands the blood and brings it to her cheek, though the prospect of marriage turns Daphne inwardly pallid. But beauty is its own wish—a wish whose power supersedes the lesser desires of the one who is beautiful. Beauty makes use of her, regardless of Daphne's will or intent. Beauty is in the face and in the body, it informs the form. It acts as an intelligence, but has no mind; it acts as a will, but has no power. Beauty conducts its work, a natural force within the one whose fate is to be beautiful, anonymous but singular, marking identity but having none itself. Beauty cannot be tamed by she who is beautiful. It is elemental. It hides paradoxically in its own showing forth. Beauty hides in vision. It is its own life, embodied in another that is also itself—and with that life, it contradicts Daphne's "deepest wish." Beauty contradicts her with herself.

3. PHOEBUS IS LOVE STRUCK

Beauty ungods the god. Cupid's arrow strikes the sun god to the marrow. Apollo sees Daphne and wants to wed her, he hopes and he longs, "but though he is the god of oracles, / he reads the future wrongly." The allegory of Cupid's arrow recognizes that beauty—and the erotic impulse beauty embodies—is thrilling. The etymology of thrilling is "to pierce, to penetrate." Beauty conducts damage on whomever gazes upon it, even if that someone is a god. To be struck by beauty is to be wounded. That wound enters into the center of the bone (not the heart); it finds in the most stonelike aspect of the human body that woundable center whose function is to create the blood the heart pumps through it. Beauty is a wound that opens paradox: it finds the blood inside the bone, and it is there, precisely there, that it harms us. It opens the lacuna in the bone, opens a space of lack in what before seemed solid, whole. It is as true for the self as it is for the bone.

But a god is no ordinary self. A god is complete, intermixed, where each aspect of self is fully interpenetrated by every other aspect. This completeness removes the gods from the human compulsion to "know thyself." The Delphic Oracle can command such in part because he himself is exempt from the process. To "know thyself" implies a partiality in the one doing the seeking—implies a blindness, a deafness, at the most intimate level of our relation to ourselves. Who we are we do not know. A god is different—is before such difficulties of self, self-knowledge, and lack. Friedrich Hölderlin senses this odd fact in "Hyperion's Fate Song":

> Fateless, like a nursing infant asleep,
>   The gods draw breath;
>   Chastely preserved
>   In modest buds,
>   Their minds are always
>   In flower,
>   And their soulful eyes
>   Gaze calmly and eternally
>   In silent clarity.

Hölderlin's vision of how a god sustains and exists in the world is a curious impossibility: the body is a bud that contains the mind's full blooming. A god exists in imminence and eminence at once. A god nurses on the air; breathing is his nourishment. As a plant thrives by sunlight, so a god thrives within the mere fact of his being—"like a nursing infant asleep," he takes in the stuff of his life without any conscious intent to do so.

Apollo is the sun god, the god of light—and like light, a god is an outward force. This dominant aspect isn't separate from his other traits. It is by virtue of light that vision occurs, even the vision of the future. Poetry is a form of sight cast into song. To hunt relies upon revelation. When Apollo is love struck he is damaged in ways he cannot perceive, for the bliss of the gods is their ignorance. He feels the pangs of desire but cannot account for the harm desire causes in him. Daphne's beauty acts upon him as a prism acts upon white light—it separates it into its component parts while still maintaining the previous unity. The god struck by desire, by beauty, by love, is a one who has become a many. The god in love grows complex as he grows empty, for emptiness is desire's work. We want what we do not have.

4. PURSUIT

Apollo burns—not because he's the sun. Seeing Daphne's hair hang unadorned against her neck enflames him.

> He sees her lips and never tires of them;
> her fingers, hands, and wrists are unsurpassed;
> her arms—more than half-bare—cannot be matched;
> whatever he can't see he can imagine;
> he conjures it as even more inviting.

This vision mimics prophetic sight, seeing that which to normal eyes is forbidden, but event is not what is revealed, nor is fate. Apollo places his own desire in his eyes, an act of will more than revelation, of imagination more than truth. When he approaches her, things do not go as the god had hoped:

> But swifter than the lightest breeze, she flees
> and does not halt—not even when he pleads:
> "O, daughter of Peneus, stay! Dear Daphne,
> I don't pursue you as an enemy!
> Wait, nymph! You flee as would the lamb before

the wolf, the deer before the lion, or
the trembling dove before the eagle; thus
all flee from hostile things, but it is love
for which I seek you now!"

Unwittingly, unwillingly, Apollo finds himself cast in the role of the
hunter. The woman he loves flees like prey before a predator. Her
lamblike, deerlike, dovelike flight forces Apollo into the role of wolf,
lion, eagle. He pursues in desire, and she flees in fright. The erotic
pursuit mimics the hunter's chase in maddening ways: the romantic
pursuit is a form of nearing that is almost indistinguishable from the
hunter's careful approach. Both end in a hoped-for possession, though
of different natures: the erotic pursuit ends in a reciprocal possession
that is also a being-possessed. The difference is that the hunter stays
silent, wants the deer to know nothing of his approach; he wants his
arrows to appear out of the stunned silence of the air. The lover pursues with words, with warnings, to set the beloved at ease, to calm, to
tame. Words are the lover's arrows, which wound the heart through
entering the ear. The wound is a form of enchantment.

Apollo is a god of poetry, and the words he sends after Daphne as
he chases her are god-driven words. That poetic power of language
is a force that nature itself is attuned to, so that the stones and plants
and beasts all respond to the lyric chord. For Daphne to flee from
words meant to slow her, to turn her around, to alter her heart in such
a way that it opens to the god she spurns, is for the god's poetic power
to fail. Poetry is introduced to the unguessed-at fact of its own failure. Apollo is cast back upon his godly attributes as a final resource
rather than a manifold manifestation of his nature; his gifts become a
means to an end, an almost human use of power, rather than the apotheosis of those powers in the visage of the god. His godly manifestation—poetry, hunter's pursuit, light, prophecy—changes from being

a pouring forth of his nature, a god's will-less outpouring of his own godliness, to becoming a fund, a resource, a strength to turn to in order to achieve a desired end, depleted as they're used. The god acts no longer like a god, needing to know his gifts in order to use them.

As he chases Daphne he worries that she'll "stumble, fall, be scratched by brambles / and harm [her] faultless legs." Worse, he knows that "I'm to blame." She runs because he pursues, and all his efforts to slow her, to calm her, to seduce her, succeed only in making her flight more urgent, more frantic.

> But now the young god can't waste time: he's lost
> his patience; his beguiling words are done;
> and so—with love as spur—he races on;
> he closes in. Just as a Gallic hound
> surveys the open field and sights a hare,
> and both the hunter and the hunted race
> more swiftly—one to catch, one to escape
> (he seems about to leap on his prey's back;
> he's almost sure he's won; his muzzle now
> is at her heels; the other, still in doubt—
> not sure if she is caught—slips from his mouth;
> at the last instant, she escapes his jaws):
> such were the god and girl; while he is swift
> because of hope, what urges her is fear.
> But love has given wings to the pursuer;
> he's faster—and his pace will not relent.

When Apollo's poetry fails, he abandons words as a means of accomplishing his desire. But Apollo's self is not his desire, nor does he contain it. His desire runs out ahead of him, a hound hunting the hare, baying out at the site of the prey, urging the god to run faster, to keep up the pace. Desire alone outstrips the speed of the god; desire alone closes the gap between love and fear of love. Desire is more godly than the god.

5. METAMORPHOSIS

Knowing that she cannot outspeed the god who chases her, Daphne prays to her river-god father: "Help me, dear father; if the river-gods / have any power, then transform, dissolve / my gracious shape, the form that pleased too well." The instant her prayer ends it comes true: "a heavy numbness grips her limbs; thin bark / begins to gird her tender frame, her hair / is changed to leaves, her arms to boughs. . . ." Where before she ran, now she is rooted.

Beauty acted within Daphne as a kind of division, working in her against her own will. Her wish is a formal wish. The answer to her plea enacts a change in her too-fair form, and the transformation that occurs unifies the chasm between her self and her beauty. Daphne's pain had been rooted in her consciousness of the difference between her inward self and her outward appearance. Form felt at odds with content. The answer to her prayer ends the agony between subjectivity and objectivity, between content and form. Beauty is a crisis, in part, because it undoes the ability to discern content from container—it is always simultaneously within the bearer of the beauty and larger than the bearer, in the same way that the beauty of a poem springs out from the confines of the poem's formal limits.

Beauty betrays what houses it—or it does so as long as no metamorphosis occurs. The end of such beauty is a miraculous violence whose work ends the crisis that birthed it. Beauty and the beautiful become one, and in doing so change shape at the deepest level, deeper than the atomic. The change occurs at the metaphoric level.

A metaphor is a form of tension created by distance, in this case, the distance between *who* Daphne is and *what* Daphne is. Apollo's desire for her is also a desire spurred and spurned by this metaphoric base of Daphne's allure. She is more beautiful for hating her beauty. But as bark begins to replace her skin, as her hair changes to leaves, as her fast-running feet become roots, as feeling is replaced by numbness (both of feeling and of thought), the division within Daphne collapses into unity. The metaphoric chasm implodes—it is as if two sides of a canyon suddenly closed, destroying the river that made it. In that implosion metaphor ceases to be metaphor and becomes instead a far stranger quality, one whose unity is not undermined by its own radiating complexity. Daphne becomes symbolic, that figure at once wholly particular and fully universal, subject and object at once. Her power is in what cannot be told apart. To be accomplished symbolically she must be destroyed metaphorically. That violence isn't one that removes one from existence but changes what that existence is. Form and content cease to be a crisis and instead become an embrace.

6. THE LOVE FOR THE LAUREL TREE

Absurd to call a god young, but Apollo is "young" in Ovid's tale. A god is immortal, and so his youth isn't related to time. His youth is some other quality in him, a hint at inexperience, a hint that, in his Cupid-born love for Daphne, Apollo is learning something, about himself or about the world in which he, omnipotent, walks. What is a lesson for a god is also our lesson, those of us who share in his attributes—that is, those of us who would write poems which also are a form of vision and pursuit.

Apollo should cease to love Daphne when she changes into the laurel tree, his desire should lessen, should cease, having met the impossibility of its fulfillment.

> And yet
> Apollo loves her still; he leans against
> the trunk; he feels the heart that beats beneath
> the new-made bark; within his arms he clasps
> the branches as if they were human limbs;
> and his lips kiss the wood, but still it shrinks
> from his embrace, at which he cries: "But since
> you cannot be my wife, you'll be my tree.
> O laurel, I shall always wear your leaves
> to wreathe my hair, my lyre, and my quiver. . . ."

Apollo's love is furthered by its impossibility. His desire continues unaltered by the risk of consummation. Instead, his desire finds in its failure a renewed momentum. In doing so, his desire ceases to act merely on his behalf, ceases to be the hunting dog yelping out to help the hunter's pursuit. His desire becomes instead a garlanded thing, a force that finds its only proof in the continued impossibility of wanting what it wants, wanting past the world's limit of what can be had. Desire wears a laurel crown, as does the god, as does the poet who practices the young god's art. Desire here meets its object, but the object has transformed—has changed, in fact, because of desire's threatening pursuit. That metamorphosis does not end desire but commemorates it and speeds it on. What changes the young god into the god is his initiation into the work of wanting.

That work undoes him. To desire removes him from his own power, it makes him suffer in ways oddly parallel to she whom he pursues. He finds himself without resource, in a kind of sympathy even though in pursuit, for his desire outruns him, chases her whom he loves, introduces the god to the impossible fact of his own incompleteness.

Poetry is birthed from such awful realization—a fact which denies the fact of one's own being, that says the self, even the godly self, is not sufficient unto itself. Poetry is a form of desire devoted to the impossibility of its own fulfillment. Its failure is crowned by the god's symbol, the laurel crown. The poet is partial; the poet is never complete. He wears a crown on his head made from the leaves of the laurel tree. The symbol doesn't complete him, but does the opposite. It incompletes the poet further, so that the poet's poem speeds out ahead, in pursuit of what he loves, nearing it closely enough that what he loves must change, must transform and take its truer shape, removed from violence, but marking that violence, where the poem barks out its location and utters its song, and the poet approaches, lustful but hesitant, as desire changes into devotion, and devotion speeds ahead, involved in its own holy pursuit.

The Indweller's Aversion:
Thoreau's Sacrificial Wonder

> Singers call men back to a time when there was no
> need of singers.

—Seth Benardete, "The First Crisis in First Philosophy"

1. THE DESCENT FROM OLYMPUS

In the morning the Muses sing the morning. The morning is not a melody separate from the music; the singing is the morning itself—not in time, not in passing—in a song that repeats daily, though a day not reduced to hours, a day not composed of time. The morning is that portion of the day larger than the day itself. The Muses sing the morning on their mountain, and as they sing, they descend. The song changes as the Muses descend. At mountaintop the song is Olympian; on the plain, the song is Titanic; and beneath the ground, the song is, as Seth Benardete, in his reading of Hesiod, says, of the "Cosmic-gods." The song the Muses sing beneath the ground is Chaos's song, is Night's song. Beneath the ground the Muses sing Earth and Eros: the beginning of the beginning: the dark morning that beneath the sunlit sphere keeps humming its midnight drone against the tuneless nothing in which no world exists. Morning is also the dark music before the sun blinks on.

The Muses' singing descent, as with the human eye looking out into the cosmos, approaches the earliest act of creation the further out they go. The song that begins in Olympian light, and the supposed order, the supposed rationality, of the Olympian rule, ends in the violent world beneath the world, a world before song which song still must sing, the world from whose darkness song first emerged, a disturbance on nothing as wind disturbs water, as water ripples out to every shore and so touches all, the Muses descend and, singing back, end in Chaos. Here, the Muses do not sing of the beginning; the beginning is their song. Then the Muses turn, and singing, ascend back to their Olympian height. Then the morning that never ends is for another day complete.

Thoreau's work in *Walden* is a morning work, a work of auroral observation, and so, too, of song. Thoreau understands that the Muses' song does not sing of what the Muses see; it is the song that casts upon those objects the light by which they are seen. Other gods forge the world, but the Muses sing it into human vision. Thoreau describes the virtue of his self-built home as follows:

> The upright white hewn studs and freshly planed
> door and window casings gave it a clean and airy
> look, especially in the morning, when its timbers

were saturated with dew, so that I fancied that by noon some sweet gum would exude from them. To my imagination it retained throughout the day more or less of this auroral character, reminding me of a certain house on a mountain which I had visited the year before. This was an airy and un-plastered cabin, fit to entertain a travelling god, and where a goddess might trail her garments. The winds which passed over my dwelling were such as sweep over the ridges of mountains, bearing the broken strains, or celestial parts only, of terrestrial music. The morning wind forever blows, the poem of creation is uninterrupted; but few are the ears that hear it.

We learn a few facts of Thoreau's vision, though *facts* seems the wrong word to describe what we learn. His house next to a pond evokes a house situated upon a mountain. The morning light lingers in the house all day. The house itself betrays time as it passes. One cannot see such light without imagination, nor hear the earth's music as it sweeps up the mountain, wails around the corner of the house, and so returns to its celestial sphere. Thoreau's house, seen in the right light, is a fit stopping place for the gods, for the Muses as they sing their song. It is a house Thoreau himself created as a resting spot within that vaster creation still ongoing. He did not create it to pause, but to participate. My hope is to show, for Thoreau and via Thoreau, what the work of such participation is—what its costs are, its "economy," so to speak, as well as what such costs purchase. The Muses descend in the morning; they descend from the mountaintop. For Thoreau, "Olympus is but the outside of the earth every where." There is, it would seem, an earth just below the earth. To put a spade in the ground is to open Tartarus. It is also to open the earth. Inside the earth there is the morning, there is the sun. "The sun," Thoreau reminds us, "is but a morning star."

2. FOUNDING

Thoreau begins his work by borrowing. He borrows an ax to cut down some pine, to provide the wood to frame the house, and returns the blade sharper than he received it. Soaking the wood in the icy water to swell it, he watches a snake dive in the hole and remain torpid in the pond. Such an uncanny moment to many men would prove a poor omen. Not so for Thoreau, whose superstition in the world allows the world to reveal to him its signs as a form of promise rather than warning. Superstition for Thoreau is not a cloudy interpretation of cloudier symbols, but an accuracy of eye that sees that the objects of the world are themselves expressive of the symbolic reality they reveal, and in revealing, participate in. Jane Ellen Harrison mocks Plutarch's mockery of such superstition:

> He deprecates the attitude of the superstitious man who enters into the presence of his gods as though he were approaching the hole of a snake, and forgets that the hole of a snake had been to his ancestors, and indeed was still to many of his contemporaries, literally and actually the sanctuary of a god.

The snake that settles torpidly down on the bed of Walden Pond reveals what Thoreau already knows, and what, in building his home next to the pond, he wishes to be neighbor of—that Walden Pond is a home to the gods, and as such, is sacred, is sacrosanct—and to trespass falsely into such sanctuary, is to be bitten by the god that protects it, that dwells within it, and to suffer that wound as a consequence of the lack of one's capacity for vision and belief. But for Thoreau, the danger isn't simply trespass. The more profound danger is that the sleeping god will not awake. Thoreau must build a morning not only for himself, but for all who dwell in the morning.

After borrowing, Thoreau buys. He purchases "the shanty of James Collins, an Irishman who worked on the Fitchburg Railroad, for boards." In April, he takes the shanty apart board by board, laying them on the grass to "bleach and warp back again in the sun." A man comes to watch him in his work: "He was there to represent spectatordom, and help make this seemingly insignificant event one with the removal of the gods of Troy." Wit aside, the allusion back to the Heroic Age, and Thoreau's identification with the Achaean army, speaks to the deepest work Thoreau sets out to accomplish within *Walden*'s pages. His work is not to desecrate the gods by destroying the sanctity of the home in which they dwell. Thoreau sees, and laments through most of his "Economy," that most of the homes in which we dwell have no gods within them. Ornaments replace the ancient idols. Our gods occupy no holy ground preserved in the house expressly for their dwelling; our gods occupy the cornices, decorate the eaves; our gods are manifested in the attempt to "put a core of truth within the ornaments, that every sugar plum in fact might have an almond or caraway seed in it." Our gods are not carved of stone, but molded of plaster. Not all idol worship is blasphemy. It is the idle worship of the idol that proves damning to our larger faith in the world, and those supernal beings the Heroic Age claims in the world dwelled, and so must dwell still—if ever a home could be built in which they could tarry.

Of course, James Collins's shanty has no such plaster decorations. James and his wife remove, too, all the belongings that filled their home, packing all into one large bundle. The "desecration" the spectator watches, and in watching, elevates the rural scene to epic importance, is not the removal of any given holy object from the house, but the removal of the walls of which the house itself is composed. The gods are not a set of statues, are not, in fact, anything positive in the sense that an object is positive—the gods here are but the space defined by walls in which dwelling can occur. The gods are not what fill a home, but the possibility that a home may be filled. In this sense, Thoreau subtly begins to shift the nature of his criticism of homes, of home ownership, from a societal harangue to a philosophical meditation. A home is the creation, through setting up the barrier of four walls, of that negative space in which a deliberate life can occur. To build one's own house by one's own hand is not only to create a space in which to live, it is also to re-create that universal process in which we live, by which we came to live. The world of things denies Chaos, denies Night—and so, too, denies morning as anything more than the opening of day whose hours can be measured by the sundial's shadows. The raising of the four walls of a house creates within this world of things a place of absence still waiting to be filled, re-creates Night, re-creates Chaos and the silence Chaos is, that soundless nothing before Cosmos bangs into being, before Cosmos utters a word.

As the Muses' descending song is also the musical recounting of those god-sparked creative forces by which the world was made and governed—from the contemporaneous Olympian to the ancient Cosmic—so too is building a house a recounting, a reenactment, of that same process, albeit on a microcosmic, human plane. It is not a morning's work, but the work that leads toward morning. Morning is Thoreau's concern; "morning brings back the heroic ages." The morning that never ends has not yet begun. There is still work to be done.

After Thoreau borrows, after he buys, he begins. To begin is to dig. "I dug my cellar in the side of a hill sloping to the south, where a woodchuck had formerly dug his burrow, down through sumach and blackberry roots, and the lowest [strains] of vegetation, six feet square by seven deep, to a fine sand where potatoes would not freeze in any winter." Digging is a labor of the hands in relation to the earth, but for Thoreau digging is more than a manual labor. Digging is also the work of the mind: "My instinct tells me that my head is an organ for burrowing." The odd anthropomorphism of the declaration equates his work with the work of the snake Thoreau watched torpid at the pond's bottom, the snake that must burrow with its head (such as the eastern hog-nosed snake does) as it has no hands, to excavate in the earth a hole in which to live. Thoreau's ideal house might be just such a burrow, dug simultaneously by hand and by head, a foundation dug into the earth with the earth as ceiling: "The house is still but a sort of porch at the entrance of a burrow." A hole is the perfection of a home.

The appeal is in finding an animal whose instinct to build is innate rather than, as is our domestic impulse, inherited by habit or by custom. Thoreau seems to be searching for those examples only the world, and not architecture, can supply, in which the act of dwelling isn't a learned activity, but an activity as natural to the builder as is breath to one who breathes. But the burrowing snake's hole and the woodchuck's burrow next to which he digs his cellar aren't the only models for Thoreau's own instinct to build. He also writes of birds:

> There is some of the same fitness in a man's building his own house that there is in a bird's building its own nest. Who knows but if men constructed their dwellings with their own hands, and provided food for themselves and families simply and honestly enough, the poetic faculty would be universally developed, as birds universally sing when they are so engaged?

The bird's song cannot be separated from the bird's work. The song is the musical expression of the nest; likewise, the nest is the formal expression of the song. The potency of the nest as a symbol is in its ability to yoke together into a single object the irreconcilable opposites of song and structure, of music and matter. The intangible and the patent collide, and the result of the collision is a nest, is a home—and a home expressly created not to house the body of the builder, but to give shelter to those builders not yet born. The nest houses creation; the nest is built in song. To sing is to sing of creation; to sing is to create that space in which creation occurs.

What links Thoreau's models for the construction of his own house, the burrow and the nest in the bower, the dwelling within the earth and the dwelling above it, is the attitude in which both are created: mindlessness. Thoreau seeks in himself the impulse to build. That impulse begins building by doing the opposite of building. He chops down, he tears apart, he digs. The first act of building is destructive. One needs to learn to make a space of nothing within something; one needs to work to begin with abyss. The work to be done requires an act the world seems to abhor even as the world necessitates it. One cannot do such work through knowledge. Knowledge is its own ornamented architecture, a system to build artificially that which Thoreau must build innately. Thoreau's economy undermines epistemology. Thoreau asks, "How can he remember well his ignorance—which his growth requires—who has so often to use his knowledge?" Ignorance is the mind's foundation, reality's basement, wisdom's cellar, the emptiness of whose depths does not simply promise the grandeur of the house that can be built in it, but far more importantly, speaks of the wonder that fills such nothingness, a wonder that is the arrival of the world into the perceptive mind. Knowledge is the architecture by which wonder and reality are severed into opposing realms. Ignorance is the emptiness in which both are one.

Knowledge, we assume, is lofty; and truth true beyond the matter of the earth that proves it so. Reason's light makes a shadow of the sun—or so those who believe in reason as the height of human under-standing would have us believe. Ignorance is base. It undermines the cathedral of human reason by putting a crack in the cornerstone that runs chaotically through the structure entire, and if that cathedral has been built without due ignorance, that is, without a foundation deep enough to warrant its height and splendor, then ignorance will bring the glory crashing down to this same earth the building, in its skyward towering, repudiated. *Walden*'s ignorance accomplishes two related works. Thoreau seeks to hammer a crack into that corner-stone, and if not bring it down, let the hammer's hollow sound be its own warning. But Thoreau does a deeper work than that necessary social critique; he digs a depth into the earth; he digs with his hands in his head. The two models Thoreau provides—the nest and the burrow—do not function as symbols in opposition to one another, though they occupy opposite realms. The nest and the burrow mark out the vectors along which Thoreau must learn to build. For every motion down, there will be a sympathetic and corresponding motion up. The builder, the maker, the artificer, the indweller, all speak of a single point—the single point a man is. "A point is that which has no part," Euclid says. But the point become symbolic rather than geometric definition, the point become wise rather than theoretical, the point become mythic rather than a carpenter's mark on a board— that transcendental point, seen from within, is also a sphere. Thoreau is just such a point in relation to himself, in relation to his home, in relation to the world. The world, too, shares the same geometry: "This whole earth which we inhabit is but a point in space." As he digs down he builds up. A life is a line spanning a sphere, a diameter. The burrow and the nest are one. Both lay tangent to the sphere that Thoreau himself has become, and in touching it, they begin to define the diameter of the indweller's own self, that line that offers a measurement of the whole person.

The nest and burrow are not endpoints. Their importance in actuality is enveloped within their symbolic importance. The symbol functions, as Emerson describes in "Circles," as those points which break through the limits of one orbit and establish the ring of another, and do so forever. The nest and burrow do not simply mark the boundaries of Thoreau's building of home and self, but are also the symbolic engines by which his work expands outward and gains its truer, if less definitive, meaning. Thoreau digs down and builds up. It is an elemental work. It expands and does not cease expanding even after the last nail has driven the last shingle into place. We must build a wall to find out that we are a circumference always expanding, and that the work of the body ends at the universe's edge—in the bird's nest in which the universe is borne, and in the burrow below the stars. Thoreau writes about this outward expansion as he digs the foundation for his home:

> What of architectural beauty I now see, I know has gradually grown from within outward, out of the necessities and character of the indweller, who is the builder,—out of some unconscious truthfulness, and nobleness, without ever a thought for the appearance; and whatever additional beauty of this kind is destined to be produced will be preceded by a like unconscious beauty of life.

Thoreau would have us note, we who in reading about his work also participate in it, also become builders ourselves, that it is not intelligence but unconsciousness that allows our work to be done. If we are to read *Walden* by its own necessary terms, then we must read it as Thoreau has built it—with our heads as burrowing tools, and build within its pages a foundation for our own dwelling. Intelligence hinders and does not help such purpose. Intelligence seeks knowledge to fill in the gap of wonder. To live unconsciously, to work unconsciously, is to dwell in wonder as one dwells in the real, never succumbing to the easy myth of facts that in explaining the world dismiss its ongoing mystery, and likewise, dismisses the mystery of he who holds in his hand the facts. Such intelligent building always ends in the dweller living outside what he has built, and he finds that in his zeal to know what he can know, he has forgotten to build a door in the wall, and can only knock upon the emptiness to be let in. Not Thoreau. He is an indweller in the world. He has built, has never ceased building, a foundation. Thoreau dwells within.

3. THE SACRIFICE OF AVERSION

Thoreau moves into his house on "Independence day, or the fourth of July, 1845." The house is not yet winter ready, lacking plaster and chimney. But the house in its symbolic structure is complete. It houses the morning light all day. The house has become a place of indwelling. The house has become an elemental nexus. Its foundation penetrates seven feet into the earth, its floor made of packed dirt lies level with the earth, and its walls holding up its roof rise eight feet above the earth. When it's finished, it's a "tight shingled and plastered house, ten feet wide by fifteen feet long, and eight-feet posts, with a garret and a closet, a large window on each side, two trap doors, one door at the end, and a brick fireplace opposite." The symmetry of the house is notable: the opposing windows, the door opposite the fireplace, the cellar's depth almost equal to the ceiling's height. Thoreau's house establishes itself on three separate strata: within the earth, upon the earth, and above the earth. In "founding" itself in each stratum, the house also unifies them. The house is the crucible in which the old elements collide again: Chaos, Earth, and Night. The life of he who lives in such a house is a figure akin to Eros—he who dwells at the point of universal consummation.

Jane Ellen Harrison relates the importance of Porphyry's noting the difference in the place of worship for differing divinities. For the Olympian gods, worshippers set up temples and altars. For the chthonic gods and for heroes, hearths. And for "those below the earth . . . there are trenches and *megara*." Each class of divinity, of power, has its own strata of worship, of sacrifice. The Olympian gods, who dwell on high, receive worship from altars that lift the material of sacrifice off the ground. Heroes and chthonic gods receive their due recognition in the fires of the hearth, built upon the ground. Darker gods are offered sacrifices in trenches or cave dwellings underground. Harrison points out that change in the place of sacrificial rites traces the transition from "under to upper-world rites." For our purpose, though, in looking at Thoreau's work in building his house, and the work that he begins only after the house is built—his sporadic reading of Homer's *Iliad* in Greek, his partial writing of *Walden,* his hoeing of beans—it's important to note that the house as he constructs it replicates each location of worship within its own structure. The house of the indweller not only replicates in its symbolic value the universe's own construction, the house also provides the grounds of worship, the grounds of reverence, to the gods who created that universe. The house built according to Thoreau's conception of architecture claims the true home is but an extension of he who dwells within it, as a turtle lives within its shell. That conception of the indweller, when tied to the symbolic meaning of the house, fuses together the act of living with the acts of faithfulness the gods demand. To live within the house is to conduct the rites of worship. Those who worshipped and sacrificed to the Olympian gods, those deities of the upperworld, ate of the food they offered, and so participated in the bounty. Not all gods live on Olympus, though. "The gods of Aversion . . . were regarded as gods that presided over the aversion of evil; there is little doubt that to begin with these gods were the very evil men sought to avert." For those gods, the gods of Aversion, different sacrifice was due.

Thoreau's wish "to live deliberately" requires the practice, almost religious in nature, of aversion. This work of aversion occurs in a variety of ways in *Walden,* each of which contains importance in its own right, but when concatenated together, prove to be the primary method by which Thoreau conducts his living experiment. Aversion, we should note, is a merciless form of economy: it forces one to turn away from the whole. Thoreau enters the woods in part to flee those philanthropic do-gooders whose virtues so infuriate him:

> If I knew for a certainty that a man was coming to my house with the conscious design of doing me good, I should run for my life, as from that dry and parching wind of the African deserts called the simoom, which fills the mouth and nose and ears and eyes with dust till you are suffocated, for fear that I should get some of his good done to me,— some of its virus mingled with my blood.

The danger of such moralizers isn't simply in their blind ethic, and their self-certainty undergirded by a lack of self-knowledge, but more profoundly, the danger is that such moralizing blows, as does the simoom, a dust that fills the senses and so suffocates them. Thoreau hates such people not because he disagrees with their moral rigidities; he hates them because those certainties destroy our capacity to perceive the world in which we live. Such doctrines derived from the religious dogma of the day condemn the person to whom their good is done to a state of dead perception, in which the meaning of the world occurs in an ethical code, not writ in stone but writ in custom, and does not occur within the world itself. Thoreau's answer is to avert, to turn away—and in doing so, shake the dust from his ears and wipe the dust from his eyes and let the dust pour back out his mouth, so that he can hear, see, and speak again. He does not do this because he is a better person than those who would "help" him. "I never knew, and never shall know, a worse man than myself." He does it because the "virtuous," like flatterers, stop one from being able to know oneself, and in doing so, stop one from knowing the world. Better to be an awful man and know oneself as such, than to be a "good" man and know oneself not at all.

In this sense, Thoreau enacts the work of aversion that Emerson, in "Self-Reliance," expresses: "The virtue in most request is conformity. Self-reliance is its aversion. It loves not realities and creators, but names and customs." Emerson's self-reliance, and so Thoreau's, turns away from social reality in order to witness and participate in the deep-set reality of the world. For Emerson, the reality of the world doesn't occur in the world. Nature is but a symbol that gives access to he who can read it, who can apprehend it, to the ideal reality in which the world hovers—an egg aloft in the ether. Self-reliance turns inward to turn outward, as if one could avert so deeply into the self that the inverse motion occurs and the self expands to its proper sphere, the limits of the universe. Emerson's self-reliance requires the recognition of the soul as a greater reality than the body, of the soul as the larger anonymous realization of character's lesser specificity. Self-reliance is the discovery of self as that unique resource whose final gift is the recognition that the self, in its truest sense, is not unique at all, but part of an ever-expanding, undifferentiated whole. Emerson's self-reliance brings us to the miraculous paradox that the soul is not contained within the body, but that the body is contained within the soul. To be ensouled, we must move outward from the self—a motion accomplished using aversion as a first step. Extreme idealism functions by denying the very grounds by which it realizes itself. Self-reliance, in its Emersonian manifestation, requires that the social self divorce itself from society, and in turning toward itself as its only company, unfold again into the ideal whole, in which the self as a unique grounds of experience dissolves into the importance of a universal reality into which it is wholly subsumed. Thoreau's self-reliance is also an aversion to self-reliance. He will not turn from the substance of the world to peer through celestial veils. Thoreau turns toward the world. His head "is an organ for burrowing."

Emerson's self-reliance is an intellectual work; Thoreau's self-reliance is a ritualized one. Thoreau enacts what Emerson theorizes. What for Emerson is a symbolic circumcision of self in relation to society, for Thoreau is the material of sacrifice. That symbol, that material, is the same for both men—it is the self. To sacrifice the self isn't to commit suicide, it is to offer one's days and the living that occurs in those days to a purpose greater than the sacrificing self can contain. A sacrificial approach to the day isn't to kill the hours that fill it, but to live within them—to use them, to work in the hours in which one has work to do, to rest in the hours when rest is allowed, to wake in the morning "and find dawn in me." It is also to lose the world by waking to it:

> Every man has to learn the points of compass again
> as often as he awakes, whether from sleep or any
> abstraction. Not till we are lost, in other words,
> not till we have lost the world, do we begin to find
> ourselves, and realize where we are and the infinite
> extent of our relations.

To sacrifice is to lose not merely the material of sacrifice, but the fact of that material. Sacrifice is the transfer of what is known into the hands of what is unknown. It does not confirm mystery in denial of fact but connects mystery to fact. Sacrifice returns to the world that darkness from which morning must emerge. Sacrifice is a form of waking.

Jane Ellen Harrison notes that the material of sacrifice changed according to the technology of the day's culture. The sacrifice of meat arose after husbandry made meat eating a norm. Sacrifices of wine became ritual after the cultivation of vineyards. The most ancient form of sacrifice corresponds to the most basic form of human sustenance: grains, and from grains, bread. One such sacrificial material is the *pelanos*:

> You first sprinkle the meal on the water, you then stir it, so far you have porridge; if you let it get thicker and thicker you must knead it and then you have oat-cake. It has of course frequently been noted that a *pelanos* may be either fluid or solid, and herein lies the explanation. When the *pelanos* is thick and subjected to fire, baked, it becomes a *pemma,* an ordinary cake. . . . A *pelanos* was then primarily the same as *alphita,* barley-meal. The food of man was the food of the gods, but the word was early specialized off to ritual use. There is, I believe, no instance in which a *pelanos,* under that name, is eaten in daily life or indeed eaten at all save by Earth and underworld gods, their representative snakes and other Spirits of Aversion.

Further, such sacrificial meals were conducted in imitation of Homeric rites, and the food the heroes in the *Iliad* ate. It's worth comparing

the *pelanos* as sacrificial meal, eaten only by the earth and the underworld gods, by snakes and "Spirits of Aversion," to Thoreau's meals
while at Walden:

> Bread I at first made of pure Indian meal and salt,
> genuine hoe-cakes, which I baked before my fire
> out of doors on a shingle or the end of a stick
> of timber sawed off in building my house; but
> it was wont to get smoked and to have a piny
> flavor. I tried flour also; but have at last found a
> mixture of rye and Indian meal most convenient
> and agreeable. . . . I made a study of the ancient
> and indispensable art of bread-making, consult-
> ing such authorities as offered, going back to the
> primitive days and first invention of the unleav-
> ened kind, when from the wildness of nuts and
> meats men first reached the mildness and refine-
> ment of this diet. . . . [A]t length, one morning I
> forgot the rules, and scalded my yeast; by which
> accident I discovered that even this was not in-
> dispensable,—for my discoveries were not by the
> synthetic but analytic process,—and I have gladly
> omitted it since. . . .

Given that Thoreau's primary reading material while at Walden was the
Iliad, his study of the ancient authorities likely ended in Homer's pages,
perhaps even with Achilles's shield, on which Hephaestus etched the
picture of a harvest feast. Thoreau's bread baking occurs in echo of ancient sacrificial rites to the "Spirits of Aversion," those dead heroes and
underworld gods whose furies and joys, whose agonies and triumphs
filled the world's morning with meaning that resonates to the pond's

edge at which Thoreau washes the flour from his hands. Thoreau's aversion turns not only from society, but also from time, also from self, and the unleavened bread scorched in the fire, the scorched bread that, along with a cup of water from Walden, serves as his daily meal, not only evokes the heroic age it alludes to, but in its repetition of ancient practices, invokes into the present that Arcadian age lost in the present world, but dwelling within it still.

Thoreau sprinkles no grain as libation, nor does he cast a portion of bread into the pond or into a crevice in the earth. He places no biscuit at the snake's hole. He eats the sacrificial food himself. Ingestion, too, is a form of economy, a form of aversion. Ingestion is the biological parallel to aversion as a philosophical practice. To eat the food of sacrifice oneself is not to make the claim of one's self as the god to which one sacrifices. Rather, to eat the sacrificial bread claims that the world one wishes to live in, and so the world one does live in, exists within the self as much as it exists without the self. To eat the *pelanos* oneself is to recognize that the power to incur evil, or the power to avert it, lay equally within the province of the self who is afflicted by, or freed from, that same evil. This is not to say that the realm of subjectivity is the limits of the world—transcendentalism, especially as derived from Emerson, is riddled by the holes of such skepticism. Thoreau's transcendentalism remains remarkably free of the taint of philosophical skepticism. Thoreau places the sacrifice of bread in the dark hole of his own mouth. The teeth that threaten to bite him are his own. The voice that promises to speak its sibylline prophecy is his own voice. More to the point, that voice promises to be his voice speaking in the voice of another living forever within him, and if in him, then in all of us. Not only is Olympus "the outside of the earth everywhere," so inside each of us lie the holy *megara*, where the shades wait for nourishment, and into whose chasms sacrifices were thrown. Thoreau, like Emerson, shares the transcendental belief that the self both contains all and participates in all. Thoreau, too, is searching for access to "the infinite extent of our relations." This discovery, though, is not an intellectual one, nor is it a philosophical one, though its overtones incline toward the philosophical. This discovery is mythic, is wonder-full. To live again in the morning that "brings back the heroic ages," one must become a hero oneself. To garner the aid of the dead heroes, one sacrifices the meals they themselves, when living, ate. When the dead hero is yourself, you eat the bread you offer.

4. Heroic Work

What is the end of such self-sacrifice? A strange nourishment.

As Thoreau eats he also feeds those "Spirits of Aversion" dwelling not only in the world, but in the world he himself is. The ongoing shade-life of heroes and spirits, beings that once performed their deeds on earth, belong not only to the earth where those deeds occurred. Such beings of Aversion dwell likewise within the human mind. As much as Achilles is the preeminent figure, in his mad sullen rage, of the *Iliad,* he is so because Homer has put the hero in the pages by which we remember him. Heroes, and the "heroic age," those men and women of the world's morning, undo the easy dichotomy between self and world, haunting the periphery that holds subject from object, inner from outer. The dead heroes' unhappiness is belonging, in death, not to human memory alone, nor to the deeper etched history of the world, but to both simultaneously. Only the transcendental self, the self-reliant self, contains the resource to hold both contraries together. Whether such work is soul-work or mind-work or body-work misses the point. The power of the self-reliant man dismisses such divisions by claiming them false. To divide is to already be conquered. To avert, as self-reliance requires, is to turn from a fractious whole (society), to a fragment whose portion is all (self). Likewise, Thoreau's self-reliance works to undo that far more rigorous dichotomy than that of body and soul, it works to undo the division between self and world, and brings us to a reality in which self and world are mutually co-containing, as Milton's angels can walk bodily one into the other without loss of identity. Self-sacrifice is a meal that feeds the selves within the self, and in reviving them to the present world, also awakes the world from its slumber. The heroes do not step forth into the day; a hero steps forth into the morning.

Thoreau's self-sacrifice results in an inexplicable doubling that occurs within self and world, and doubles self and world, without ever manifesting that doubleness in actual division. Thoreau becomes a two that remains a one. The vaunted accuracy of his senses magnifies into a kind of double-vision, double-hearing—not synesthesia, that confusion of two senses into one, so much as a single sense operating biologically and metaphorically at once. Thoreau can now see in echo, hear in echo, and those echoes precede the reality of the object from which they resight and resound. "The echo is, to some extent, an original sound, and therein is the magic and charm of it." Thoreau can now see the footprint that comes before the foot. He enters a state of "negative capability" not as a poetic method, but as an unavoidable consequence of resuscitating the mystery of the world. Thoreau begins to live in what Keats calls the "Penetralium of mystery" which, unlike Keats's notion, reveals verisimilitude rather than being dispelled by it.

> A lake is the landscape's most beautiful and expressive feature. It is the earth's eye; looking into which the beholder measures the depth of his own nature. The fluviatile trees next the shore are the slender eyelashes which fringe it, and the wooded hills and cliffs around are its overhanging brows.

Thoreau is shocked into an accuracy all the more accurate for its inaccuracy. That is, Thoreau's eye has become metaphoric. He sees the world reveal itself in terms of what it is not, but that negativity posits itself as a deeper insight into its reality. Thoreau lives by a lake that is one of the countless eyes of the world. The eye on whose brow he lives is remarkable for the clarity of its vision. Thoreau's eye is the same eye, and for the doubleness to maintain its symmetry, as in a painting by Arcimboldo, we must see the lashes around Thoreau's as "flags and rushes" pushing through the lid's rim's alluvial soil, that bed of vision. The image contains greater startle. The lake as an eye implies a sentience within the earth that functions as does our own. It watches, and then it knows. The world sees itself being seen. To know so is also to know oneself as seen. The hierarchy of subject to object falls apart, and the epistemology built on that division collapses with it. What is left is the world and the self, each caught in the shock of the other's gaze.

The hero's work occurs in just such a world—a world invested, because affected, by the events that unfold upon it. The hero in this sense is but one of the varied produce of the world, a phenomenon as natural and miraculous as the wheat husk growing heavy with germ, and the hero's actions are evidence of his ripeness. The hero is he who tills the earth, be it by sword or by hoe—a destruction whose end is plenty. It is not a field of grain the hero plants; he plants us. The hero at death is a seed dropped back into the furrow he himself carved, splendor buried in the sillion. We are the fruit of that seed, or we can be, if we seek the name of our own roots. Achilles. Hector. Hercules. The hero is an agricultural form. The hero replenishes the world he replicates. The hero, as Stanley Cavell notes, tends his beans. The opening paragraph of "The Bean-Field" testifies not only to the heroic transformation Thoreau's "sacrifice of Aversion" results in, but the doubling consequence of that transformation.

Meanwhile my beans, the length of whose rows, added together, was seven miles already planted, were impatient to be hoed, for the earliest had grown considerably before the latest were in the ground; indeed they were not easily to be put off. What was the meaning of this so steady and self-respecting, this small Herculean labor, I knew not. I came to love my rows, my beans, though so many more than I wanted. They attached me to the earth, and so I got strength like Antæus. But why should I raise them? Only Heaven knows.

Not only does Thoreau become Hercules in his labor, he becomes the monster Antæus, whom Hercules killed by lifting off the strength-giving ground. As Thoreau's digging his foundation had a simultaneous countermotion that built upwards, uniting burrow and nest, so his epic transformation occurs in light and darkness, in hero and monster. The hero is no hero without the dark mirror image of the monster that the hero must defeat. That hero he is must defeat the monster he is. The battleground is within the self fighting the battle. The agony is self-agony. As the counterpart to Emerson's "Self-Reliance" is his "Experience," wherein the consequences of his idealism come to harrowing light, his grief that he cannot grieve at the death of his son, his realization that "an innavigable sea washes with silent waves between us and the things we aim at and converse with," so this double-creation of hero and monster resounds as the consequence of Thoreau's self-reliant aversion. Emerson ends in Idealism's silent, griefless trap; Thoreau ends in myth's monstrous self-grappling. Emerson becomes separated and ever more singular; Thoreau becomes mythic and occupied. Emerson, in one of his rare moments in which his voice sounds defeated, says "It is very unhappy,

but too late to be helped, the discovery we have made, that we exist."
Thoreau's discovery, though, is not too late, for his discovery leads
toward morning. Existence is not a defeated end, but a heroic beginning. Thoreau as Hercules, Thoreau as Antæus, Thoreau as Achilles
destroying the weedy Hectors in the bean-field, discovers not only
that "we exist," but that all that has existed still exists: heroes and
leaves, monsters and Muses. There is but one leaflike pattern struc-
turing the entire world.

> You find thus in the very sands an anticipation of the
> vegetable leaf. No wonder that the earth expresses
> itself outwardly in leaves, it so labors with the idea
> inwardly. . . . The feathers and wings of birds are
> still drier and thinner leaves. . . . The very globe con-
> tinually transcends and translates itself, and becomes
> winged in its orbit. Even ice begins with delicate crys-
> tal leaves, as if it had flowed into moulds which the
> fronds of water plants impressed on the watery mir-
> ror. The whole tree itself is but one leaf, and rivers
> are still vaster leaves whose pulp is intervening earth,
> and towns and cities are the ova of insects in their
> axils. . . . The Maker of this earth but patented a leaf.

Thoreau, in nourishing within himself the figures of the heroic age,
begins to live within that age. He does so as himself, but he is no
longer singular, no longer a figure of easy solitude. He is Hercules
and Antæus fighting over a row of bean leaves, but the hero and
the monster are but leaves themselves, unfurling within the leaf that
Thoreau is, proving the single patent form that is the world. There is
a tree from which no leaf has ever dropped. Those leaves feed upon
the light they shield us from: a morning that refuses to become time.

Thoreau's heroic work doesn't end with the "small Herculean labor" of hoeing his beans, that field that ripens in the sun but does not age in it. That work is writing *Walden*. A field and a book both occur in lines that end in the margins. "Writing is," as Stanley Cavell says, "a labor of the hands." *Walden,* then, is a heroic labor. Writing, too, is a work of doubling. Words and heroes share a phenomenological principle: both are double, both are twice themselves. Words name the world because words cannot be the world. Language suffers a Typhonic condition. Typhon's great threat wasn't located merely in his monstrous power, but in his ability to imitate any voice, even the voices of the gods. A writer is not Typhon, but is, inevitably, one of Typhon's children—those that still walk the earth, in ever greater number, which Hercules in his labors didn't know to destroy. Mimesis then is not an outdated mode of literary theory, but the crisis of the writer's condition. To speak is to imitate that which is, and in imitating, double. A word is a weak monster gaining strength, like Antæus, from the ground it walks upon. As much as Thoreau becomes Hercules and Antæus while tending his beans, he becomes Homer and Typhon when tending the field furrowed in *Walden*'s pages. This transformation is not spoken, because it is unspeakable. The monster here feeds upon the very weapons used to kill it. Writing, too, occurs in agony. Nor does silence destroy such a monster—silence unleashes the Furies.

Language is an ideal monster. The distance between name and world thrusts words into a sphere in which reality begins to occur above the earth of which it speaks. Within that distance thinking occurs, philosophy occurs. The absence language encompasses makes writing the fertile ground of doubt, requires a writer to find a way to use language against itself, to create metaphors, to create conceits that momentarily close the gap the writer's project attempts to bridge. Language's particular failure isn't simply a sign of futility or defeat, it also a sign of vitality, of creativity, of resource. Language requires thought because it makes possible thinking. But Thoreau's work is not to think; his work is to burrow, to build, to dwell. The page is a place of living, in solitude, yes—but not only in solitude. The page, like the house, is the structure of invitation, of hospitality. Thoreau's hospitality while at Walden is a strange one:

> One inconvenience I sometimes experienced in so small a house, the difficulty of getting to a sufficient distance from my guest when we began to utter the big thoughts in big words. You want room for your thoughts to get into sailing trim and run a course or two before they make their port. The bullet of your thought must have overcome its lateral and ricochet motion and fallen into its last and steady course before it reaches the ear of the hearer, else it may plough out again through the side of his head. Also, our sentences wanted room to unfold and form their columns in the interval. . . . I have found it a singular luxury to talk across the pond to a companion on the opposite side. In my house we were so near that we could not begin to hear,—we could not speak low enough to be heard; as when you throw two stones into calm water so near that they break each other's undulations.

Words expressing thoughts are bullets, and then they are stones. They can possess a deadly momentum. They can break the surface of the water. Words, and so the thoughts words compose, are for Thoreau shockingly solid, shockingly real. Drop a word on the page and the page like a pond will ripple. With swift economy, Thoreau conflates house and page and pond into a single phenomenon. He does so and removes himself to a far corner. We need not, like those visitors from town he'd rather not see, leave an odd token of our visit—a strip of birch bark with our name as a calling card. Thoreau has asked us to stay, and built a house beside a pond in which we're welcome to hurl our thinking around without fear of destroying the place in which we think. The house is built beside a pond, but the house is the pond. He writes of his house and writes of the pond on a page, but the page is the house that is the pond. How still the dark waters are when one stands on the white margins. Do you hear the echoes in the water? Do you hear the loon laughing when she swims up from the depths? Do you hear the laughter echo on the water? Step in. Thoreau has stepped in. The page is water we can breathe. A hero always enters the underworld. The page is a depth. The hero always enters a depth, and returns from the shades with the living. Words, too, are shades, are shadows. Enter them. The hero enters them and invites you to join him. The hero enters into words, he does not only speak them, and returns from those shades with the living.

5. WONDER

Thoreau enters a mythology into his economy. It is a mythology of loss, of the lost:

> I long ago lost a hound, a bay horse, and a turtle-
> dove, and am still on their trail. Many are the travel-
> lers I have spoken [with] concerning them, describing
> their tracks and what calls they answered to. I have
> met one or two who had heard the hound, and the
> tramp of the horse, and even seen the dove disap-
> pear behind a cloud, and they seemed as anxious
> to recover them as if they had lost them themselves.

Stanley Cavell, writing about this strange, mysterious passage, notes that its importance may not be locatable in an interpretation of the symbols of the three animals, but in positing for the reader the loss of them. Thoreau gives us an absence. What is missing, for those of us who have glimpsed the creatures once, opens in us the same awareness of loss Thoreau himself is experiencing. This loss leaves its tracks. We can follow what is missing. What we've lost hasn't left us bereft; what we've lost has put us in motion. This little myth makes clear the nature of the myth *Walden* itself is. *Walden* is the myth of recovery, the return to presence. To read *Walden* is to seek not so as to discover, but to reclaim, to recover. To read *Walden* is to seek not what hasn't yet been, but to search again for what already is. Heroic writing is this work of recovery—for the hero does his work within myth. When the hero is the writer of his own myth, when he is Homer and Achilles both, the book ceases to be the recording of mythic events, but is itself the myth it records. Thoreau becomes dizzyingly, dazzlingly, doubled. He is the hero writing the book in which he is the hero writing the book. The book records the thing it is. Thoreau writes a myth of recovery; he is recovering himself.

Thoreau builds his home on Walden's shores because he has been to Walden before. He is digging his foundation in a unique location in which recovery is the paramount quality for his real-estate choice.

> When I was four years old, as well I remember, I was brought from Boston to this my native town, through these very woods and this field, to the pond. It is one of the oldest scenes stamped on my memory. And now, to-night my flute has waked the echoes over that very water. The pines still stand here older than I; or, if some have fallen, I have cooked my supper with their stumps, and a new

growth is rising all around, preparing another aspect for new infant eyes.

In returning to Walden Pond, Thoreau returns to the location of his
earliest memory. He returns to when he saw the world with "infant
eyes"—and the work of recovery *Walden* heroically represents, is to
see again with those same eyes. The infant eye opens on wonder.
What the infant eye opens wondrously upon etches itself into the
child's mind as memory. Thoreau plays a music over the water that
awakens the echoes of those memories. Words will not do it. Music
enchants those echoes back into existence, and then the echoes speak
for themselves. The echo arrives before the word; the past tense speaks
before the present. What words Thoreau hears are the first words he
spoke on seeing Walden Pond as a four-year-old, words that in seeing
the world wondrously realize it. To return to Walden and live on its
shores returns Thoreau to the location of first awareness, when, in
miracle and wonder, he saw a portion of a world and spoke it to himself for the first time. Walden Pond repairs the language by which it's
described, for it is that location that presented itself to initial utterance, wherein words didn't repeat the figure of the pond in Typhonic
imitation, but in naming the pond, participated in its uniqueness. To
return to Walden's shore is to return to a place in which language re-
gains its morning light—where a word itself emits the light by which
it sees the world it names. The semantic crisis of sign and signified
implodes back into the singular star whose light lights all. Then to
speak is to speak in the morning. The morning is when a word is a
form of wakefulness, when a word is a form of wonder.

Walden Pond resonates wondrously in Thoreau not only by virtue
of his childhood connection to its waters. Part of *Walden*'s epic un-
dertaking occurs in a return through memory to a place before experience has laid down the cornerstones of knowledge. *Walden* compresses

two years of living into a narrative that seems to occur in a single year, but Thoreau is doing a more profound work on time than compression. The nature of memory-work in *Walden* finds expression again, a century later, in William Carlos Williams's lines from "The Descent":

> Memory is a kind
> of accomplishment
> a sort of renewal .
> even
> an initiation, since the spaces it opens are new places
> inhabited by hordes
> heretofore unrealized,
> of new kinds—

Thoreau's aversion creates a horde within him—bearing that complexity of hero and monster serves as his initiation into a world he once belonged to, and to which he longs to return. It is not enough for him to see with his own eyes. Eyes must stare out through his eyes. When that horde exists within the self, memory ceases to be a relation between the present moment and all that does not qualify as present. The past returns in a wonder that removes it from time. The written word is the essential vehicle for contradicting time. The word speaks across centuries, bridging the reader's present moment with the present moment of the writer, and in connecting those centuries, obliterates them. Time is a wall words know how to knock down. Words, too, contain in them a history each utterance repeats, though our access to that history is questionable—it being so much longer lived than us. As Thoreau finds in Walden the location of his earliest sight and so earliest speech, so each word promises within itself a Walden of its own, pure waters within the binding edge of a word's form. A word, in the mythology of *Walden,* contains within it a path back to its own necessary infancy—that place (for time seems already a disruption of such presence) where the name named. Language, to steal from Wallace Stevens, is our "imperfect Paradise," pointing back through itself to perfection. Memory leads to "new kinds" of experience—not the heretofore unexperienced, but the return to an initial experience that has yet to cease occurring.

Walden Pond, in the sun's morning-star light, is the center of the world. There may be many such centers; every point on the globe may be such a center. But for Thoreau, there is only the center that is Walden Pond.

> Perhaps on that spring morning when Adam and Eve were driven out of Eden Walden Pond was already in existence, and even then . . . it had commenced to rise and fall, and had clarified its waters and colored them of the hue they now wear, and obtained a patent of heaven to be the only Walden Pond in the world and distiller of celestial dews. . . . It is a gem of the first water which Concord wears in her coronet.

Caroline Walker Bynum, in *Metamorphosis and Identity,* writes: "Not merely a physiological response, wonder was a recognition of the singularity and significance of the thing encountered." Thoreau recognizes Walden Pond. Its singularity is one of the fundamental facts of the world, unchanged since Adam and Eve left paradise to begin their toil in dust—to work in their own bean-fields. To drink Walden Pond's waters is to slake the throat's time-parched thirst. Thoreau works to return to the world from which he's never departed, to find in words a path of wonder. He insists that we must do the same—at least, those of us who are capable of such work, we readers of *Walden.* We must

be heroes wrestling with the monsters we are. We, too, must be initiated. The continuing astonishment *Walden* provides its readers results
in its unique relationship to the wonder it evokes. As the book and
pond and home are in *Walden* one, to read deep is to drink deep is to
dwell long. A reader is kin to the loon that swims through a blue sky
whose element is water and not air. The writer shares the same plum-
age. The loon lives in the depth of pages, emerging on the surface to
laugh at what he's found true. Within the bound edge of the page, the
shore's white margins, reader and writer continuously appear only to
dive under again—as if the writer's sky were the reader's water, and
the reader's pond were the writer's air. We exchange elements, laughing at the absurd moment in which both, for an instant, gain sight of
the other. It is a mockery we must follow if we are to become readers
capable of recognizing the wonder Thoreau brings us. We must learn
to put aside sense and knowledge to regain our infant hold on the
elements: to grasp the dirt of which we're made; to drink the water
of which we're composed. To do so requires our ignorance; it also,
Thoreau in his own mockery (mock-epic, mock-etymologies) reminds
us, requires our humor.

Walden is an ignorant book. If it were not, it would destroy with
knowledge the wonder it evokes out of unknowing. There is in *Walden*
no such evanescence, where the wonder of the world departs ever to
the horizon. In *Walden,* the horizon stands still when we stand still,
approaches when we step toward it. "Once it chanced that I stood
in the very abutment of a rainbow's arch, which filled the lower stratum of the atmosphere, tinging the grass and leaves around, and daz-
zling me as if I looked through colored crystal." *Walden* is seen from
within the rainbow's light. The pure eye is the pot of gold that recognizes no real value can be coined. To see so requires a work Thoreau
presents to his readers by living that work himself. The results of such
aversion, such sacrifice, such unleashing of heroic hordes within the

self, is a remarkable and necessary doubling, through whose accumulating selves the world in its singularity can be seen. Caroline Walker Bynum writes, "Every view of things that is not wonderful is false." Thoreau, I think, would agree. The heroes in him would nod their heads. Thoreau would nod both his heads: "Sometimes, also, when the ice was covered with shallow puddles, I saw a double shadow of myself, one standing on the head of the other, one on the ice, the other on the trees or hill-side." Thoreau sees in his reflection on Walden Pond his true size. He is exactly twice himself.

He has doubled into wonder.

Wonder is the fact that the world has never ceased to be real.

The Nightingale's Drought, the Nightingale's Draught:
On Metaphor, Magic, and Symbol

Rainbird, to what far place
are you crying?
The world is overflowing
with that water.
The water where sound and sea
divide. . . .

—Kabir

I. DROUGHT

Drought threatens both the world and the poem. In the world, drought destroys plants and the animals that eat them, destroys the generative capacity of seed and stem and leaf; drought grows dust. Drought in the poem grows dust in the mind. The image of a plant may be dropped on the page, but the plant on the page is a form of dust, it lacks a vital principle, and desiccates the mind it enters. Experience plants such ill harvest. In *Songs of Experience,* Blake writes of his pretty rose tree:

> A flower was offered to me,
> Such a flower as May never bore;
> But I said, "I've a pretty rose tree,"
> And I passed the sweet flower o'er.
>
> Then I went to my pretty rose tree,
> To tend her by day and by night;
> But my rose turned away with jealousy,
> And her thorns were my only delight.

Drought here is a form of denial. Blake's rose tree mimics his own action, his own turning away from the first offered rose. He turns from the singular flower to flowers abundant on the tree, but the abundance turns away. To turn one's back on one beauty removes the capacity not only to be nourished by another, but to nourish another. To turn one's back on one rose, "offered" though we don't know by whom, is also to dismiss the beauty of the roses one owns. Drought is a condition in which, due to our own actions, due to our own negligence, we delight in thorns—whose only blossoms are the drops of blood they let. A tree grows in this drought, as Blake sees in "The Human Abstract":

> The gods of the earth and sea
> Sought through nature to find this tree,
> But their search was all in vain.
> There grows one in the human Brain.

Perception creates of the outer world an inner one. Skeptics delight in the tree that growing down the lane takes root behind the eye.

Reading, too, is perceptive work—but a work, compared to direct perception, that doubles the skeptic's delight. The tree that takes root in the mind is first "the tree that takes root in the mind"—not the natural object, but the linguistic one. The tree that grows "in the human brain" is not an image from the world itself, but one evoked by a use of language conveying information the world may or may not be able to offer. When we read we see a tree we cannot see, should we look up from the page for proof. That tree we see is a dusty tree. In the crisis of drought, we water it with dust when we read. It grows in drought and its fruit is drought.

Drought is the fact that the imagination works even when it's dead; Blake's thorns keep our eyes open. T. S. Eliot's *The Waste Land* is a poem whose crisis occurs in such drought:

> Here is no water but only rock
> Rock and no water and the sandy road
> The road winding above among the mountains
> Which are mountains of rock without water
> If there were water we should stop and drink
> Amongst the rock one cannot stop or think
> Sweat is dry and feet are in the sand
> If there were only water amongst the rock
> Dead mountain mouth of carious teeth that cannot
>   spit
> Here one can neither stand nor lie nor sit
> There is not even silence in the mountains
> But dry sterile thunder without rain
> There is not even solitude in the mountains
> But red sullen faces sneer and snarl
> From doors of mudcracked houses
>   If there were water

And no rock
If there were rock
And also water
And water
A spring
A pool among the rock
If there were the sound of water only
Not the cicada
And dry grass singing
But sound of water over a rock
Where the hermit-thrush sings in the pine trees
Drip drop drip drop drop drop drop
But there is no water

This long excerpt from "What the Thunder Said," the final section of *The Waste Land*, combats its own aridity with its waterlike motion, with the hermit thrush's waterlike song. One word from a line almost always repeats in the line that follows creating an eddylike whirlpool of sound and image within the linear motion of each line. The poem's structure mimics the very element that's missing in the landscape, missing from the mountain: water. The poem moves as a river moves, but that work of imitation doesn't end the drought—it exacerbates the recognition of the lack of water. What we feel formally we feel forcefully, undeniably. Nor does the hermit thrush's "drip drop drip drop drop drop drop" call forth the patter of rain, or the leaky faucet, the song incants. Eliot gives us the mimicry of water as if to call water forth, "but there is no water." Where there is no water, there is no place to "stop or think," there is "not even silence," there is "not even solitude." Drought isn't simply a condition of the climate, it is a dearth whose deathly difficulty spreads contagiously into all those who dwell in the waterless world. Drought is also a human condition.

Water is the most basic element of generation, the source of life. Without it, we would not be; with its disappearance, we will cease to be. The human manifestation of drought in *The Waste Land*, mimicking the generative necessity water symbolizes, is the erotic. Much of the deepest sorrow in Eliot's poem is revealed not in the lack of the sexual act, but in the meaningless of it. "The nymphs are departed," repeated twice. Tiresias knows. He suffers what he sees, and so should we:

> The time is now propitious, as he guesses,
> The meal is ended, she is bored and tired,
> Endeavours to engage her in caresses
> Which still are unreproved, if undesired.
> Flushed and decided, he assaults at once;
> Exploring hands encounter no defence;
> His vanity requires no response,
> And makes a welcome of indifference.

Tiresias, in Eliot's poem, is the "old man with wrinkled dugs." Unlike the blind prophet's mythic narrative—in which, after striking apart mating snakes, he transforms from man to woman, and after many years living as woman, finds the same snakes mating and, separating them again, returns to his former gender—Tiresias here is hermaphroditic, man and woman simultaneously, an erotic whole. But *The Waste Land* is a land of drought. Tiresias is old, impotent. He foresees meaningless erotic encounters. He has "foresuffered all / Enacted on this same divan or bed." What Tiresias sees he also experiences. The prophet's vision is unique in that the future event is experiential in nature, and consequence occurs in the prophet before the event occurs in the world. To see Tiresias, this "old man with wrinkled dugs," is to witness the consequence of drought. We cannot judge, as he cannot judge: we are participants in the world we see. We too have "foresuffered all"; we too, as the "small house agent's clerk" does, grope our way downstairs, "finding the stairs unlit." That staircase figures one experience of drought.

"Where do we find ourselves?" Emerson asks. "In a series of which we do not know the extremes, and believe that it has none. We wake and find ourselves on a stair; there are stairs below us, which we seem to have ascended; there are stairs above us, many a one, which go upward and out of sight." Tiresias sees us descending down those stairs, each step opening onto a drought-struck world, each step opening on the "the violet hour, the evening hour," where the "typist home at tea-time, clears her breakfast" and looks out the window at "her drying combinations," and awaits the man who, in having sex with her, increases in them both their barrenness. The desperate series seems infinite. Tiresias serves not only as witness and victim and perpetrator all at once, he also represents the withering presence of the ancient world in the drought-struck world that is current. The old prophet still sees, still lives, but cannot warn. Drought disconnects the vitality of the ancient world to the current world without severing the connection. The myths are present, and they are useless.

Not useless, perhaps—the myths decorate the crisis. A woman, aristocratic, it would seem, sits in her boudoir, applying creams, applying "her strange synthetic perfumes," brushing her hair. A fire burns in the room. Candles burn. The candle smoke rises to the ceiling:

> Huge sea-wood fed with copper
> Burned green and orange, framed by the coloured
>   stone,
> In which sad light a carvèd dolphin swam.
> Above the antique mantel was displayed

As though a window gave upon the sylvan scene
The change of Philomel, by the barbarous king
So rudely forced; yet there the nightingale
Filled all the desert with inviolable voice
And still she cried, and still the world pursues,
"Jug Jug" to dirty ears.
And other withered stumps of time
Were told upon the walls; staring forms
Leaned out, leaning, hushing the room enclosed.
Footsteps shuffled on the stair.
Under the firelight, under the brush, her hair
Spread out in fiery points
Glowed into words, then would be savagely still.

An erotic residue, as of smoke's dark smudge on a ceiling, clings to the atmosphere. The woman sitting in her chair "like a burnished throne" seems to be preparing herself for an amorous night—an encounter that, if not desired, seems not to be dreaded. Again, the prelude to intimacy is indifference. She brushes her hair out. The brush holds the hair as it moves through it, extending it out to its full length, where the tips catch fire with the flame's light and glow into words—then the brush moves past the tress, and the hair falls back, silent and still. Whose words glowed in the "fiery points" of her hair? The only vocalization in the scene comes not from the living woman, but from the wooden one, carved into the mantel, singing her nightingale's song: "Jug Jug." Other unnamed forms lean out from the walls into the room, other mythologies exert a silent presence, lacking song, lacking words to name themselves. Hair is a curious symbol. It grows out from the head and so bears a relation to the thoughts the head contains—is somehow, even if imperfectly, expressive of them. Hair marks the inward nature of the person. Hair, seen in a certain light, is expressive of the life out of which it grows. Those words glowing at the end of her hair, those "fiery points" that seem to belong to the "leaning forms" as much as to her, whose utterance, could the words be uttered, would not only name the unnamed figures on the walls, but in naming them return them to some semblance of life. The source of that life isn't within the forms themselves, nor is it within the words that may name those forms. The life is within the mind that thinks those words, and in thinking them, in speaking them, sustains the objects of that thought, of those words. Brushing her hair gives image and motion to the invisible processes of her thought, and the collapse back into stillness and silence is emblematic of a parallel collapse in her mind.

We have only Philomela singing her song. It is doubtful Philomela's "Jug Jug" is audible within the woman's chamber. The poem names the song not because it is being sung, but because Philomela has been named, and by naming the myth carved into the mantel, the poem has access to the song that is that myth's consequence. The song itself is silent, and that silence is one of the most bitter ironies within *The Waste Land*. Eliot lets the nightingale's song sing out through the desert of Thrace, as if to point out that in the ancient world, though not in ours, song still filled the vacuum atrocity created. "But here there is no water"; but here there is no song. Philomela, raped by her brother-in-law, her tongue cut out to stop her from telling of the crime, who learned to speak with her hands, who embroidered the tale of her rape into a cloth sent to her sister Procne who exacted a revenge equal in horror to the horror committed upon Philomela, killing and cooking her own son, serving the son to the father for dinner, and who, being chased by the murderous Tereus, is transformed by the gods, as all three are, into birds. Mute Philomela becomes the nightingale; Procne a swallow; Tereus a hoopoe. Philomela presides over the boudoir, a household god whose blessing recognizes a horror of which she cannot speak. The myth encircles the room, promising a transformation that in *The Waste Land* seems impossible. In the room, in the heartless preparation for the heatless erotic encounter, Philomela's tongue is cut out again. The atrocity isn't rape. The atrocity is indifference. In a world of drought, where no moment can come to meaning, where sex itself is the least vital of human acts, the nightingale becomes again the tongueless woman, who watches over horror that never looks like horror, the everyday lifelessness of the living who act like the dead they unknowingly envy. Philomela watches and cannot sing her lament.

Her lament, her song, returns in "The Fire Sermon":

> Twit twit twit
> Jug jug jug jug jug jug
> So rudely forc'd.
> Tereu . . .

Fragments of song and story stitch together the body of *The Waste Land*. The poem as a whole is remarkably free of metaphor and the transformations metaphor attempts to enact. The poem feels like Ovid's *Metamorphoses* without the possibility of metamorphosis. Water, too, is the transformative element. It sprouts the stonelike seed into the sunlike flower. It is the lack of this transformative element that makes of *The Waste Land* a wasteland. Metaphor ceases to be able to function in a world in which transformation is impossible. Eliot instead undertakes a waterlike activity in the absence of water. As a river divides the land it simultaneously connects, so Eliot connects fragment to fragment: "These fragments I have shored against my ruins." These fragments encircle the nameless speaker of the poem in the same way that Philomela carved on the mantel, and the other unnamed mythic personage encircles the nameless woman in her boudoir. One of the explanations for the radical shifts in tone and location *The Waste Land* presents its readers with is that the fragments are held together by the riverbeds of the missing rivers, held together by drought. Crisis in *The Waste Land* is connective. Eliot shores together locations of meaning without claiming meaning in them; he shores them against the ruins of himself—not the possibility of self-failure, not his *ruin,* but against his *ruins,* the crumbling architecture of the grandeur the self once was.

"If there were water . . . If there were rock / And also water / And water / A spring / A pool among the rock / If there were the sound of water only . . ." then the jagged leaps, the stepping without explanation into new voices, the tone of omniscience that doubts its own knowledge, all the difficulties that indelibly mark *The Waste Land* would be solvable, soluble. . . . "But there is no water." A river allows us to live at the point of division. Without the river the place of division isn't seen as division—the boundary exists but is not seen as a boundary. We step over it into a new country or ancient city, into the underworld, or into the bedroom, and do not know how we arrived. We just know we are there, inexplicably, in the Waste Land. We don't have a metaphor by which to leave, only a metonymy by which to continue on our ceaseless travels. There is, or there can be, a song in this desert: "Jug jug jug jug jug jug." The nightingale all night can sing. Her song makes melody of an object that carries water. Inside the song we can hear both the exasperated cry and the solution to the crisis. To sing, perhaps, makes of one's voice that form which can contain the water that is missing. The song is not a rain song, but an emptiness that can hold the rain if it comes; not a river, but what one dips into the river to slake one's thirst. It is not magic, but the form magic might occur in. That song is formed not by avoiding horror but by enduring it. That song is Philomela's legacy; it is also ours. It would seem the solution to *The Waste Land*'s crisis, to the drought—both elemental and erotic—would be water, would be life. But nothing is simple in *The Waste Land*. In *The Waste Land*, remember, we must "fear death by water." What seems to give us the promise of life also promises to take it away. To end this drought, which is our drought, we must seek other means.

2. RAINMAKING AND METAPHOR

Emptiness is full of itself. Drought is a form of emptiness, meteorological and metaphorical at once. It is a crisis in the poem and a crisis in the world because both forms of the crisis affect the human. The human response to finding the ground dry, to finding the mind dust-filled, is to seek some means of solution. In the crisis of drought, the ancient instinct is to find water. When there is no water to be found, the ancient instinct is to force water to arrive. The rainmaker, the public magician, would begin his ceremonies in the promise of darkening the sky with clouds. Different cultures practiced different methods of controlling the rain through magic—but a central principle unifies the variety. James Frazer calls that principle "sympathetic magic," the old belief "that like produces like, or that an effect resembles its cause." Magic is practical work based on the perceived notions of the world's laws, the world's operation. Magic works through creative imitation—a replication on the human plane of a larger work in the world or the universe. Magic seeks to bridge, through imitation, through repetition, the human and the nonhuman. As Frazer says, "the same principles which the magician applies in the practice of his art are implicitly believed by him to regulate the operations of inanimate nature." As above, so below: the magician's chant.

In Eliot's *The Waste Land* the crisis the magician would solve is the crisis of drought. Frazer's *The Golden Bough* exerted great influence on Eliot's poem but did not lend the poem a magical solution to its central problem. Eliot's poem, as remarkable as it is for its lack of metaphor, is remarkable too for its lack of magic. There is no magician among the living and the dead who populate *The Waste Land*. One finds only fortune tellers, the cold-ridden Madame Sosostris and her "wicked pack of cards." One finds only impotent, ever-suffering, ever-seeing Tiresias. To be able to see the future is a different species of magic than the ability to affect the present. The magician is as blind to the future as the prophet is blind to the present. The magician cares for the dry acre of this season's field, not the field that threatens to be barren next season. The practicality of magic is the understanding that, save for rescuing the present moment out of present crisis, there will be no future to foresee. Drought in *The Waste Land* isn't only the lack of water, but the lack of a magical solution to that lack of water. Worse, the condition that lurks within *The Waste Land* sees modernity as a world in which the vestige of magical ritual remains— "That corpse you planted last year in your garden, / Has it begun to sprout? Will it bloom this year?"—without the possibility of magic as a result of that rite. The form of magic practiced in *The Waste Land* is an empty form, a thoughtless habit, a gossip among the day's topics for conversation. But it wasn't always so.

The magical varieties of rainmaking are numerous, sometimes shocking, often beautiful in the bent of their logic. One example from Frazer:

> In time of severe drought the Dieri of Central
> Australia, loudly lamenting the impoverished state
> of the country and their own half-starved condi-
> tion, call upon the spirits of their remote prede-
> cessors, whom they call the Mura-muras, to grant
> them power to make a heavy rain-fall. For they
> believe that the clouds are bodies in which rain

is generated by their own ceremonies or those of neighbouring tribes, through the influence of the Mura-muras. The way in which they set about drawing rain from clouds is this. A hole is dug about twelve feet long and eight or ten broad, and over this hole a conical hut of logs and branches is made. Two wizards, supposed to have received a special inspiration from the Mura-muras, are bled by an old and influential man with a sharp flint; and the blood, drawn from their arms below the elbow, is made to flow on the other men of the tribe, who sit huddled together in the hut. At the same time the two bleeding men throw handfuls of down about, some of which adheres to the blood-stained bodies of their comrades, while the rest floats in the air. The blood is thought to represent the rain, and the down the clouds.

The Dieri ceremony continues with even greater elaboration, including the carrying of heavy stones many miles and placing them high in trees, as well as the breaking apart of the ceremonial hut by the men of the village who, in this process, forbidden to use their hands or legs, must break it apart using only their heads. As Frazer notes, the blood represents rain and the down clouds, but the representation by which the ceremony works contains even greater depth than Frazer's insight opens. The bleeding men also act as clouds, dropping blood into the men gathered in the hut in the ground. The roof of the hut is the roof of the sky, and the two bleeding men who walk around it act as clouds themselves, raining down blood on those within the earth—both literally and figuratively. The men sitting in the hole in the earth occupy the position of seeds. The blood-rain falls down on them to reenact the work the rain must accomplish if the tribe will survive the drought. It must not only rain, but the rain must cause the seeds in the earth to sprout. The down that represents the clouds changes its figurative nature when it lands on the blood-stained bodies, the rain-stained bodies, of the men in the hut. When the men emerge the downy feathers are no longer clouds but are now the downy wisps of a plant gone to seed. The head—in a magical way of thinking—is the sky of the body. The men use their heads to break apart the hut in which the first magical transformation occurred. The hut, too, was a sky and an earth—a whole macrocosmos limited by the extent of the hole the hut was built within. But this magic, to be effectual, cannot be restricted to the container in which the magic occurs. The men destroy the hut with the firmament of their own bodies. The head now serves as a complex symbol. It is sky, it is cloud, but it is also flower—a flower gone to seed. The men break apart the hut with the sky of their heads, with the clouds of their heads, with the flowers of their heads. They break the hut apart so the magic in the hut can occur in the world.

Other magical methods of making rain are less elaborate if similarly striking: the pouring of water on a young girl adorned with flowers; a woman throwing a stranger in a river; dragging a plow against the current through a stream. In many cultures, Frazer notes, twins possess a magical power adept at working on rain.

> The . . . power of influencing the weather is attributed to twins by the Baronga, a tribe . . . who . . . inhabit the shores of Delagoa Bay in South-eastern Africa. They bestow the name of *Tilo*—that is, the sky—on a woman who has given birth to twins, and the infants themselves are called the children of the sky. Now when the storms which generally

burst in the months of September and October have been looked for in vain, when a drought with its prospect of famine is threatening, and all nature, scorched and burnt up by a sun that has shone for six months from a cloudless sky, is panting for the beneficent showers of the South African spring, the women perform ceremonies to bring down the longed-for rain on the parched earth. Stripping themselves of all their garments, they assume in their stead girdles and head-dresses of grass, or short petticoats made of the leaves of a particular sort of creeper. Thus attired, uttering peculiar cries and singing ribald songs, they go about from well to well, cleansing them of the mud and impurities which have accumulated in them. The wells, it may be said, are merely holes in the sand where a little turbid unwholesome water stagnates. Further, the women must repair to the house of one of their gossips who has given birth to twins, and must drench her with water, which they carry in little pitchers. Having done so they go on their way, shrieking out their loose songs and dancing immodest dances. No man may see these leaf-clad women going their rounds. If they meet a man, they maul him and thrust him aside. When they have cleansed the wells, they must go and pour water on the graves of their ancestors in the sacred grove. It often happens, too, that at the bidding of the wizard they go and pour water on the graves of twins. For they think that the grave of a twin ought always be moist, for which reason twins are regularly buried near a lake.

If all their efforts to procure rain prove abortive, they will remember that such and such a twin was buried in a dry place on the side of a hill. "No wonder," says the wizard in such a case, "that the sky is fiery. Take up his body and dig him a grave on the shore of the lake." His orders are at once obeyed, for this is supposed to be the only means of bringing down the rain.

Twins possess power because twins are nature in excess of itself. Twins represent a bounty that cannot be accounted for, as if one should plant a single seed and from that seed two plants grow. Drought is a condition of lack; twins counter that lack with evidence of nature's impossible abundance. To water the graves of the twins, wherein their bodies lie as seeds lie in the earth, serves to remind nature of a process countless times reenacted in both the human and vegetable world— the springing forth of more than is needed, the miracle of plenty.

Human twins aren't the only twins possessing curious power. Language, too, is born into the human mind twinned. Every word has its twin: that object its syllables name. A word insists that an object exists in the world to which its name applies. A word conjures that object in the mind even when the object itself is absent. That image in the mind is another twin. To think magically risks the absurd belief that to speak can call forth a missing object into presence. Elegy as a poetic mode refuses death as the loved one's final departure. The poem calls back the person from the shades. Eurydice follows Orpheus as long as he sings, as long as he doesn't look back to see if his words work—as long as his song waters the twins. The world follows the magical word, catching up with it, bringing itself back into sunlight, back into presence. When there is no world, words conjure one.

Beyond the beauty of the rainmaking rites recounted above lurks a poetic principle still latent in poetic practice today. Sympathetic magic, as Frazer illustrates it, works as metaphor works. The magician, like the poet—whose genius, as Aristotle says, is marked by the ability of his eye to find resemblances—works by seeking a solution to crisis through the work of metaphor. The work of metaphor, simply put, finds resemblances within dissimilar objects or conditions. Words possess metaphoric power on a number of levels. As Emerson says, "Language is fossil poetry." Emerson encourages us to think of poetry as living language: "Every word was once a poem." The daily use of language, words of commerce and habit, words of work and small talk, maintain a vivid (if hidden) connection to their original utterance, in which to name an object likewise invoked that object back into being. A speech that accomplishes its daily task of communication maintains a connection back to the original relation with the world of which each word is born. The poem lurks within plain speech. The promise of poetry, like the promise of magic, is to turn the stone back to life (the stones that listened to Orpheus sing), to put a body again on the fossil. Language is revelatory only when it is connected to the real—a connection which language itself severs. The non-poetic use of language, the custom that covers the eyes with sight preconceived, impacts the living poetry of the word and, pressing words beneath the accumulating layers of habitual speech, ossifies it. A stone is a world of drought. A poem, as does the Baronga wizard, commands us to find the fiery grave of the twins and pour water on it. That arid grave, for a word, is itself. It is a grave we speak. Our breath can utter the simoom, or our breath can utter the monsoon. The solution to the crisis can only be found within the crisis itself— such is the harsh wisdom poetry offers those who devote themselves to its work. One must learn to write, one must learn to read, so as to water the grave, so as to unite back into lividness the twin that any given word is. Metaphor is the work of finding simultaneously the world attached to the word and the word attached to the world. It reconnects the twins it nourishes.

That metaphor becomes a necessary means of rescue from crisis—that song must rescue being back into itself—implies that a chasm has opened a distance in that which had no crack in it before. Metaphor is not simply the crisis of finding the world severed from the language meant to evoke world, it is likewise that critical condition in which language becomes merely self-uttering, a use of words in which words speak only to themselves—not world, but a linguistic effigy of world, a hollow image. At the recognition of such severance, both the poet and the magician begin searching for, as Wordsworth puts it in the preface to the *Lyrical Ballads,* "the accuracy with which similitude in dissimilitude, and dissimilitude in similitude are perceived." The Dieri and Baronga ceremonies recounted above are magical examples of metaphoric work—the rainmakers create their magic through finding similitude in dissimilitude, and dissimilitude in similitude. Their magic is our metaphor. The genius of metaphor, the genius of the magician, is to find within resemblance a method of cinching shut that distance between the world that is and the world that should be. Drought is a sign that in the world a proper order has gone awry. The magician and the poet react to that understanding by finding a method, through metaphor's magical connection of like with unlike, to bring the rain that likewise signals that the world is functioning. Both metaphor and magic attempt to make the world that is only like the world the world that is itself the world. Out of comparison metaphor and magic seek unity. The world is always a distance from itself—a canyon gapes in the sphere. Then magic begins its ceremony, then poetry begins its incantation, and the world draws shut its chasm and becomes the world. Magic and metaphor seek to collapse the world back into its true sphere.

Then comes the rain. Then the seed splits. Then the green tendril twists upward through the dirt. Then the blossom fattens. Then the flower opens. Then the bees awaken. Then the flower is abuzz. Then the pollen is taken. Then the bee is flowerlike. Then the flower is earth's version of the sun. Then the flower is yellow like the sun. And when the flower is yellow like the sun, when likeness again has asserted itself as the primary mode of relating world to universe, of relating word to world, then the sun burns hotter, then the sky grows cloudless, then the flower withers, and the fertile land grows sere, grows into waste-land, and then we are in drought. Then the next ceremony must be performed. Then the poet begins again her poem.

3. SYMBOLS AND CIRCLES

Metaphor closes a distance by capturing a likeness within unlike-ness and incanting that difference shut. Metaphor's work, though, is undermined by its own engine: unlikeness. The whole that meta-phor creates suffers from the schism of its own dissimilarity. Within metaphor absence always threatens to reassert itself, always promises to split apart along those lines of unlikeness by which it's built, the world that had been drawn back into completion. Metaphor, though, does not always serve only metaphoric ends. Metaphor, at least that form of metaphor which cannot be discerned from magic in its deep-set nature, begins a related but different work in the poem and in the world: it attempts to reassert the symbolic. The symbol, as the poet and classicist Anne Carson writes in *Eros the Bittersweet*, has an im-portant derivation:

> The English word "symbol" is the Greek word
> *symbolon* which means, in the ancient world, one
> half of a knucklebone carried as a token of identity

to someone who has the other half. Together the two halves compose one meaning.

Where metaphor identifies through misidentification, symbol accomplishes a different, if related, work. Symbol, too, collapses a distance, and the end of that collision is meaning. That meaning is housed in identity, in recognition, of bringing two halves, seemingly complete in themselves, together into an actual whole. The symbol is powerful because the symbol reunites the world into its identity as world. The symbol promises completion: what we thought was whole was only half, and there exists, if we can find it, if we're patient, the corresponding half. When the halves meet then the world is as it was. Symbol promises return. We return to a world where there is no drought. There is no drought because the world is complete. There is no lack of rain; there is no lack of thought. There is no difference between rain and thought. To think is to water the world. The mind in the symbol is precipitate.

The mind in the symbol is also on slippery ground. Emerson gives voice, gives vision, to what it is to live in such a world:

> The eye is the first circle; the horizon which it forms is the second; and throughout nature this primary figure is repeated without end. It is the highest emblem in the cipher of the world. . . . We are all our lifetime reading the copious sense of this first of forms. . . . Our life is an apprenticeship to the truth, that around every circle another can be drawn; that there is no end in nature, but every end is a beginning; that there is always another dawn risen on mid-noon, and under every deep a lower deep opens.

Whereas Carson defines symbol according to its ancient and actual use, Emerson approaches symbol in a far different, far more ideal manner. Carson sees in the symbol that material that betokens identity—a whole always composed of parts. Emerson sees in the symbol a philosophy that springs through identity into possibility. Our lives are not simply apprenticeships to the truth that around the circle of our lives another circle can always be drawn; our lives are an initiation to the possibility that we can always shock ourselves out of our particular orbit and leap to a further one. The means of accomplishing such a leap—a leap which opens "my eye on my own possibilities"—is located within the symbol itself. To learn to read symbols isn't to learn to see the future, but to see that the future has already occurred, is already present, is already in place. The future—to that eye capable of reading the cipher of the world—is not an issue defined by time. The future is a question of degree:

> We all stand waiting, empty—knowing, possibly,
> that we can be full, surrounded by mighty symbols
> which are not symbols to us, but prose and trivial
> toys. Then cometh the god, and converts the stat-
> ues into fiery men, and by a flash of his eye burns
> up the veil which shrouded all things, and the
> meaning of the very furniture, of cup and saucer, of
> chair and clock and tester, is manifest. . . . All that
> we reckoned settled shakes and rattles. . . .

We see symbolically when the veil of habit is burned from our eyes. Then each of us is Plato. We see that any given object participates in a reality vastly greater than itself, and that, paradoxically, it contains within itself. In the symbol there is a terror—that terror is a form of momentum, of potential energy, that learning to see the symbol as such releases. We spend our lives as apprentice to the objects we live among; we are always being initiated into the world. A symbol says I am what I seem and am more than I seem. A man, too, is a symbol. A woman, too, is a symbol. Metaphor covers a distance. Better said, metaphor draws the horizon close to the eye. But when metaphor's vitality wanes, the reader of metaphor is most often left standing on the same ground with the horizon reeling back to its old post at the world's edge. Our pockets are full with clichés that offer no sustenance for the journey we're told we must undertake. A symbol is a different matter—or promises to be. A symbol is the accomplishment of what metaphor attempts to magically conjure into reality. The symbol is not a species of magic—in the realm of the symbolic, magic is unnecessary. The symbolic world is a world of identity, not of unlikeness. In the symbol, where there is dust there is rain to water it.

A symbol's relationship to distance differs essentially from metaphor's relation to distance. Carson outlines the work of the symbol as a wandering through untold amounts of space that ends in two halves becoming once again whole. Implied in that connection is that the two halves, the two knucklebones, are whole when joined because they were once joined within the living body that bore them. The symbol is a return to lividness. That living realization of the symbol's nature contains within it the distance the symbol crosses on its way toward completion. A symbol is that impossible form that contains within it the infinite distance that threatens to tear it apart. The two knucklebones are akin to two bowls traveling toward one another over vast realms—save that the bowls don't simply move through space, they gather it into themselves as they cross it. To imagine it fully, we must see space as physical in its emptiness rather than simply empty. In the symbol distance is a nothing that exists, a "nothing that is." Within the symbol, when its two halves meet, the distance crossed in each half is contained within the whole—"the very furniture," the very objects of the world, of daily life, the "chairs and clocks," cease to be settled objects, but "shake and rattle." They shake and rattle because within them exists a spring shaking and rattling. That spring's energy is a result of the distance contained within the symbol itself, the necessary distance crossed in order to bring the symbol into existence. A symbol is an object with a latch. To read the symbol is to release the latch and find oneself propelled across the distance of which the symbol is made. We draw a circle around our old orbit.

"Literature," Emerson writes, "is a point outside of our hodiernal circle, through which a new one may be described." To learn to read likewise is to learn that the sphere of one's mind is a wider circumference than previously could be thought. We achieve in ourselves what objects achieve in themselves, at least when the object arrives with the force of the symbolic: "The life of a man is a self-evolving circle, which, from a ring imperceptibly small, rushes on all sides outwards to new and larger circles, and that without end." The celestial spheres served as a poor model for the universe, but serve as a profound model for that universe each person is unto him or herself. The larger we grow the more emptiness we contain. Emptiness is a primitive engine, a soul-like quality, a spring. Our lives' apprenticeship makes us disciples of the symbol—or can. We end with what Coleridge calls the "philosophical imagination," a means of reading that captures emptiness as possibility:

> They, and they only, can acquire the philosophic imagination, the sacred power of self-intuition, who within themselves can interpret and understand the symbol, that the wings of the air-sylph are forming within the skin of the caterpillar; those only, who feel in their own spirits the same instinct, which impels the chrysalis of the horned fly to leave

room in its involucrum for antennae yet to come.
They know and feel, that the *potential* works *in*
them, even as the *actual* works on them!

The gift of the symbol's emptiness resides in the potential of what wings may there grow. The symbol is a means of flight. The question the symbol asks is: where will we go?

4. DRAUGHT

Dust fills the drought-struck mind, clogging the channels of perception, of thought, numbing sensibility. It causes, as Keats says in "Ode to a Nightingale," one's heart to ache. Drought is a lack, a form of unwilling forgetfulness. To be stricken with drought is to wonder, as Keats wonders, what causes this ache notable for its lack of pain:

> My heart aches, and a drowsy numbness pains
>> My sense, as though of hemlock I had drunk,
> Or emptied some dull opiate to the drains
>> One minute past, and Lethe-wards had sunk . . .

What he hears, what does not end his numbness but exacerbates him into the feeling of his lack of feeling, is the nightingale singing from the "beechen green" in "full-throated summer ease." The nightingale, as Eliot heard it, sings in the desert of Thrace: "Jug Jug." That ancient song, its own utterance an onomatopoetic connotation of that object which carries water or wine, is the same song to which Keats listens. The nightingale's song in *The Waste Land* serves as allusion not solution. The nightingale sings whereas Philomela was forced into silence—and Philomela and the nightingale are one and the same. The nightingale's song serves as a reminder of the ancient world's divine rule of compensation that in *The Waste Land* has lost its balance. For Keats, too, the nightingale sings an ancient song—a dryad's song that serves as conduit back to the ancient world. The mortal bird sings an immortal song—a song unfettered by the affliction to self that mars human singing into self-expression. The nightingale's night-long melody never succumbs to the accident of meaning anything other than what it is: a music that sings in the dark, a music that keeps one wakeful.

Keats hears this song and wishes for a "draught of vintage!" That wish is a complicated wish. The initial sense is a desire for a jug of old wine to carry one back to the earth out of which the wine was made, the earth in which it was stored. But "draught" is a word whose etymology connects it to motion, to being pulled. Likewise, "vintage" carries in it a vestige of age, of the ancient. What Keats wants from the nightingale, the desire the nightingale's song elicits within him, is not simply a strong wine under whose influence Keats may be transported to the ancient world the song evokes, but likewise, by that same song, to be pulled by it back to that age, that Arcady, the bird's melody promises still exists. The wish is to ingest and so escape. To escape, one must follow the song to its source. The nightingale is not the source of the nightingale's song—the bird only sings the song, the inherited melody, which sang its tune to ancient ears just as now it sings its tune. The bird belongs to time, as does the poet who listens to it sing. The song exists in time but does not belong to time. The nightingale's "Jug Jug" sings open the tense within which it exists: the present. It is a present tense that bridges the ages of the world. The bird's song opens a door in that now that never ceases being now.

"Ode to a Nightingale" flits between a metaphoric work and a symbolic one, attempting to find an end to its crisis through both

interrelated, but differing, tropes. The immortality of the nightingale's song wakes Keats from his senselessness. He listens as if dead:

> Darkling I listen; and, for many a time
>   I have been half in love with easeful Death,
> Call'd him soft names in many a musèd rhyme,
>   To take into the air my quiet breath;
> Now more than ever seems it rich to die,
>
> To cease upon the midnight with no pain,
>   While thou art pouring forth thy soul abroad
>   In such an ecstasy!
> Still wouldst thou sing, and I have ears in vain—
>   To thy high requiem become a sod.

The world is without light. Keats is himself the dark in which he listens. He wishes for his "quiet breath" to be taken by death into the
air. Quiet breath carries no sound, no syllable, no song. The song
he hears the nightingale sing would still be sung without his ear to
listen. It is a song sung within the midst of death: all vision gone,
darkness within and without. Only the ear keeps the mind alive.
The song enlivens him—enlivens in him what likewise in him sings.
All form is mortal coil. The bird that sings will die. (It is worth noting that Keats, so taken by the bird's song, metonymically replaces
the song for the bird—"immortal bird!"—as if the nature of the
song had overwhelmed the nature of the bird, and rather than song
dwelling in the living bird, the bird dwells within the living song.)
The poet that sings will die—even now, is dying. The poem on the
page is itself a mortal form until a reader picks it up and hears in her
own ear its tune, sees in her own eyes its world. Only the song capable of rupturing form with the intensity of its own melodic thrust

staves off the deadening work definition always threatens to do. To sing is not to be immortal, but to recognize that whose genius is to ignore the mortal fact no mortal can ignore. To sing is to become that genius.

Both metaphor and symbol offer a means to become that genius. Both offer means to draw closer to genius's otherness, that other which genius is. Keats hears himself in the nightingale's song. He hears himself not as himself, not as one "full of sorrow / and leaden-eyed despairs," but as the wider, deeper, more anonymous self that sings beyond self-expression. Genius sings outside the self—and he who sings must depart in order to catch up to the song. To do so requires a damage done in the self, a lack of definition, a lack of sufficiency. Keats writes about this poetic condition of selfhood in his famous letter to Richard Woodhouse on 27 October 1818:

> As to the poetical Character itself, (I mean that sort of which, if I am any thing, I am a Member; that sort distinguished from the wordsworthian or egotistical sublime; which is a thing per se and stands alone) it is not itself—it has no self—it is every thing and nothing—It has no character—it enjoys light and shade; it lives in gusto, be it foul or fair, high or low, rich or poor, mean or elevated—It has as much delight in conceiving an Iago as an Imogen. . . . A Poet is the most unpoetical of any thing in existence; because he has no Identity—he is continually in for—and filling some other body—The Sun, The Moon, the Sea and Men and Women. . . .

The poet is a person with a lack of personhood. To bring the point closer to our concern, the poet is one-half of a knucklebone whose matching half is the world. The poet—at least the poet who is not a type of the "egotistical sublime," rather a poet shattered by the dissimilitude he is attentive to—seeks completion in that which he is and yet is not. Identity occurs outside the self. What keeps Keats from death in "Ode to a Nightingale" is the nightingale's song, which sings to him as if an ode to himself. It sings: in me you are complete. The nightingale's song casts out a line in the dark, a line that connects throat to ear, a line that marks a distance. The work of the ode is to find a means to close that distance, to become the bird that sings, and in doing so, rescue oneself into identity. Symbol promises identity. It seals the self to the other that completes the self. It makes of partialities a whole. Eliot remarks on a similar sense of the "poetical Character" in "Tradition and the Individual Talent":

> What happens is a continual surrender of himself
> as he is at the moment to something which is more
> valuable. The progress of an artist is a continual
> self-sacrifice, a continual extinction of personality.

That "extinction of personality" undoes the boundary of self and makes it adhesive. The poet's "I" becomes a plea for a means of approach to anything in the world that says back to him "you." The nightingale's song sings to Keats. It sings over the course of its whole melody; it sings through the midnight dark in which "I cannot see what flowers are at my feet"; it sings through death's likeness one word that never is a word: you. To hear the song is to die in a different way than to die in this world of "the weariness, the fever, and the fret." To die in song is to extinguish the partial self in order to die into the complete one.

That complete self is always more than singular. To become so requires a leap. Keats asks the bird to "fade far away." He demands, or pleads (the emotional ambiguity of the tone masks the nature of the imperative) the nightingale to leave so that he can conjur in himself the same departure:

> Away! away! for I will fly to thee,
>   Not charioted by Bacchus and his pards,
> But on the viewless wings of Poesy . . .

The duplicity of "Away! away!" reveals the double work the command must accomplish if Keats is to be rescued from the deathly world. "Away!" feels to be the only truly vocal moment in the poem, as if the poet himself was shouting to scare the bird deeper into the forest. The second "away" seems silent, seems self-spoken. What connects the two is the taut line of the song itself—that line that connects the alien parts, that promises, as symbols promise, a completion of self beyond the boundaries of self, a home in flight, a return to the world beyond death, where rain refuses drought, where draught pulls one to Arcady. Keats, too, lives in a wasteland he longs to leave. But Keats fails, he falters, his fluttering ends in confusion if not distress. He listens more than he sings:

> The voice I hear this passing night was heard
>   In ancient days by emperor and clown:
> Perhaps the self-same song that found a path
>   Through the sad heart of Ruth, when, sick for home,
>   She stood in tears amid the alien corn;
>   The same that oft-times hath
> Charm'd magic casements, opening on the foam
>   Of perilous seas, in faery lands forlorn.

The song charms windows open and the view through the casement is the "faery land" across the "perilous seas." When the song becomes magical, the crisis reasserts itself. When Keats loses his symbolic sense, the metaphoric sense takes over. He is left, painfully, confusingly, in the vagaries of similitude and dissimilitude—a world indistinguishable from dream. He is "forlorn," abandoned in the midnight world he sung himself wings to fly from. Almost sung. Almost singing.

> Forlorn! the very word is like a bell
> To toll me back from thee to my sole self!

The line connecting bird to poet, that line of music, that melody that was a destiny—that fate falls apart. The result is a return to "my sole self." It is a self in crisis, in drought—a self in a world in which "thorns were my only delight." A thorn is one remedy for numbness. A thorn floats in Lethe and stabs the throat of he who'd drink such a draught. A thorn gives us pain to wake us up. But Keats doesn't wake up. He is abandoned in between worlds, caught in the chasm magic creates when it departs. A sole-self lost between a dreary world and a fairy world. The pain in the poem is not so much that position as it is the loss of a world that denied both of the extremes the poet finds himself caught between. The symbolic world—the world of the present tense, of wonder, of now—differs from both the numbing world Keats likens to death and the "faery land" infused with magic. The poet finds himself in between, abandoned by the song that promised to complete him. He is a sole-self that is a self less than complete: a knucklebone seeking the other half to come to full identity. "Fled is that music:—Do I wake or sleep?" To be forlorn is to find oneself in a world where there is no difference between waking and sleeping. A song can prick the ear into wakefulness—if a song again will come.

5. LAST WORDS

The magical use of nightingale feathers does not solve drought. The ancient Greeks ate the flesh of the nightingale to stay awake. The nightingale conjures wakefulness. Wakefulness is the solution to the final crisis of Keats's poem. The nightingale keeps him awake.

The Waste Land ends with the Thunder speaking "peace that passeth all understanding."

And of Blake's flower? There is only the mystery that precedes the poem's first line: Who offered him the flower that May never bore? Someone offered him the flower, and may have—for each of us—more flowers in store.

INTERLUDE: MEDITATIONS

I. Typhonic Meditation

Ralph Waldo Emerson considered the mind to be volcanic in nature. The thought, ever since encountering it, appealed greatly, even if it resisted my understanding almost completely. The volcano is a conduit from the earth's molten center up through the earth's crust, and then pierces into the sky. Its geological form parallels a notion of mind: that conduit between the molten unconscious, the walkable surface of the waking self, and the ideal forms the mind thinks toward, hovering in the ether, outside of the world. But that parallel feels too akin to a school-grade teacher placing a transparency outlining the structure of the mind over the outline of the structure of a volcano she had forgotten to remove after the last lesson, on earth science, was done. It wasn't until a variety of other readings dovetailed in my mind that I began to grasp at some semblance of what Emerson's insight might mean.

For the past three years, I've been reading and rereading Proust. As awful as it is to say, given the length of *In Search of Lost Time,* it seems Proust is one of those authors who can be encountered in his full originality only by returning to the books already read. Rereading replaces anticipation with expectation. There is no longer the question of what will happen, only the half-remembered sense of what is soon to come. Rereading becomes an activity that occurs in time in a strange way: one has the sense of the moment of the page one is on, and the historical sense of all that has preceded. But the rereader has the gift of foresight, a kind of vision that has already read the un-turned pages, a gift of a sort of prophecy, which senses the future as something already lived. Of course, that intricate weaving of time, in which memory complicates present realization, in which expectation is formed by the secret work memory always does, the way we most often see "with the eye," rather than "through the eye" (to steal from Blake), is the ongoing wonder of which Proust is writing. Our vision, and so our memory which shapes that vision, is very seldom simply our own, simply of the moment of perception. When one does see, it is revelation—and time ceases to exist: the madeleine in the lemon tea, the hawthorn flowering, the ivy-clad church. But, Proust says, we seldom see. We think that we see . . . we think what we see . . . and our thinking is volcanic.

When Plato walks with Phaedrus down the middle of the river to-ward the deep grass below the trees where they will talk, when Plato follows the beautiful young man with the scroll of Lysias's written speech tucked within the sleeve of his robe, when Plato, famed for his control, for his lack of passion, seems enflamed equally by the beauty of the boy and the intoxication of language, he asks an astounding question: "Am I a monster more complicated and swollen with passion than Typho, or a creature of a gentler and simpler sort, naturally a part of some divine, and not monstrous, dispensation?" Typho, or Typhon, the monster Plato fears he might be (in a question he quickly makes rhetorical, shifting Phaedrus's attention away), is a monster with one hundred serpent tails for legs, and one hundred serpent heads. Typhon's monstrosity and strength isn't located simply in his body. Typhon, through those hundred serpents' mouths can speak in countless voices, can imitate every sound—can speak the language of the gods in the voice of the gods. Typhon threatened Zeus, threatened to overpower Olympus. Zeus, in fierce battle, trapped Typhon in a cave beneath the volcano Aetna—whose eruptions result from the monster's rage. Plato fears he is such a monster because Plato sees that he does not know himself. He fears that in being Typhonic he is no single self, but multiple selves, a hundred selves, each speaking in his own voice, simultaneously, making a din of identity. Plato's fear is Proust's material: the self that is never singular, never certain. The Typhonic self.

Typhon lives in a cave beneath a volcano. Emerson claims the mind is a volcano. There is a cave below the mind, two caves, through which the world enters the mind. In those caves lives a monster. That monster is Typhon. The monster in the cave names the world as it enters the brain, names the people in the world as we see them, talk to them, think about who they are, who we are in relation to them. And Typhon gives each thing, each person, no single name—when the monster speaks, he speaks in a hundred voices. Those voices chant upward into the molten rock of the mind, that repository of knowledge and memory that forms experience into a fiery pool. The breath from the monster's voice cools the molten rock, casts it into the convective current upwards into the mind, into consciousness, shaping what it is we think we see. When the world seems definite to us it may be a monstrous moment. To have a volcanic mind is also to have a cavern below the volcano. A monster may live in that cavern. A hero's work is to slay such a monster, but for the hero to do so, he must know what the monster is. He must know who he is. He must know that he is not the monster he's trying to slay. He cannot, in his own volcanic mind, ask the question: What kind of monster am I? But for those of us with volcanic minds, there may be no other question to ask. What kind of monster am I?

II. On Verdant Themes:
Toward One Sentence in Proust

1. IVY LEAVES AND TREE LEAVES

A tourist to its own intricacy, thinking looks at itself. The mind is both a church covered in ivy and the agent of attention that attempts to see through the verdure to the stone. The mind is its own subject. A church marks a world, it does not make a world. A church's steeple points heavenward, instructing the eye to turn away from the sensual earth, instructing the mind to concentrate on ideal forms, on thoughts, on truth. The church steeple points away from the earth on which it's built, and then the ivy creeps over it, reclaims it, pulls it back toward the earth it seems to refute. The mind thinks itself away from the world, and then the world encroaches. The ivy climbs over its thinking, a nervous system whose root is rooted in the dirt.

The church of the mind builds within itself another structure: the apse of knowledge, the altar of knowing. To think is a faithful activity devoted to reason—or so the rational think. The rational inherit the location of their faith; they inherit the architecture of their thought. The structure of the mind, that ivy-covered church, is built according to the blueprint others provide. A book is one such blueprint. The stories painted in glass are another such blueprint. But then the ivy blocks the light and the stories go black. A disorder exerts itself on order: the organic structure of the ivy contrasting the architectural order of the building. But the ivy doesn't simply mask the church— it also reveals it, it also translates it. The mind that thinks about the world, and in thinking about it claiming it for itself, is likewise claimed by the world of which it thinks. The ivy says: You are mine. To the mind, to the church, the ivy says: You are mine.

To think is to attempt to draw conclusion from resemblance. The church-clad in ivy, found in the town of Carqueville, exists both as its own entity and as a mirror to the person whose mind thinks about it, whose eye sees it: "that a projection of leaves was really the contour of a cornice, I had to keep constantly in mind." The "I" who must keep the ivy-translated church "constantly in mind" is the narrator of Proust's *In Search of Lost Time*—that narrator that is both Proust and not Proust, that narrator who contains within himself a host of other selves. Mme de Villeparisis has taken him to Carqueville to see the church "clad in ivy" on a day trip from Balbec. The ivy-covered church reawakens in him an awareness of mystery materialized on the carriage ride home, when he sees three trees whose pattern he feels he has seen before but cannot place. "I gazed at the three trees, which I could see quite clearly; but my mind suspected they hid something on which it could have no purchase, as our fingertips at the full stretch of our arm may from time to time barely touch but not grasp objects that lie just out of reach." The mind, too, is a many-fingered thing: a building that grasps. But some change has occurred in the definition of knowledge, of reading, of mind, in the course of this day whose time passes between viewing the ivy-clad cathedral and unexpectedly seeing these three strangely familiar trees.

Both moments share a leaf-covered principle, though only the first is revelatory. The ivy leaves reveal the church even as they cover it. The leaves of the trees reveal only their own pattern; they cover nothing; the structure they surround is the emptiness through which the branches jut. The three trees hide their formal nature, the knowledge upon which they are built. There is no memory in the center of the trees, only the sense of memory; no meaning, only the sense of meaning. That they exist is their wonder. The narrator knows how to see through the ivy to the church beneath, though he must remind himself of his own intelligence to do so, must remind himself that he recognizes what he sees. He cannot read the three trees as he can read the leaves of a book: they offer no content. They are recognizable as trees but not as events. They maintain their secrecy. They do not speak. "I watched the trees as they disappeared, waving at me in despair and seeming to say, 'Whatever you fail to learn from us today you will never learn. If you let us fall by the wayside where we stood striving to reach you, a whole part of your self that we brought for you will return forever to nothing.'" That fatefulness of this day trip with Mme de Villeparisis revolves around Proust's exposure to this nothingness that the trees, in their impossible evocation of meaning that can never become meaningful, grant him.

The mind, like nature, abhors a vacuum. As light pours into a black hole, so intelligence pours into nothing: it cannot escape the gravity of the lack of an object. The threat of nothing creates the uncanny sense that one might not be living the life one thinks one is living. It creates alternatives out of uncertainty: "I had to ask myself whether this whole outing was not just some figment, Balbec merely a place where I might once have been in my imagination, Mme de Villeparisis someone out of a novel, and the three old trees nothing but the solid reality that meets the eye of the reader who glances up from a book, his mind still held by the spell of a fictional setting." The sentence just quoted enacts the fear it speaks of: the narrator, who begins in the certainty of his subjective self, that certain life of saying "I," has by the sentence's end become a "he." The mind looks at itself as it thinks and a chasm occurs. The doubt-filled elegance of Descartes's *I think, therefore I am* has, in Proust, lost its subjective anchor in the sea of its own subjectivity. The *I that thinks*, over the course of the narrator's carriage ride to Carqueville, results in a *he that is,* or a *he that might be*—with the added difficulty that *he* and *I* might be the same. In Proust, doubt riddles the pronouns. By the time he listens to the trees admonishing him as they disappear for not learning their secret, it has become apparent that the *I* never obeys its own limit, but leaps into the silence of others, the silence of trees, and in speaking for them, undoes the certainty of itself. Doubt, in Proust, is a different figure than in Descartes. The self is never reduced into singularity; the self is paradoxically, or inversely, reduced into multiplicity, reduced into endless strains, like musical themes, of possibilities. We are caught in the consciousness that promises to free us. It's hard to remember that the planet's orbit is also a noose around the neck. What is it, we want to ask, that he—Proust or the narrator that is Proust—failed to learn? What had the trees to teach him? He hears them speak to him, but whose words do they speak? The three trees speak his own words. Why? Because he could not bear the nothingness of noting their silence. Against the silent other that exists, against that existence so undeniable it makes us question the reality of our own experience, our own existence, against that silent nothing the leaves of the trees cover, we add our own voice, and comfort ourselves with the thought that we are their secret, that their secret is ourselves.

What do those trees reveal? That we do not know who we are.

2. Girls and Roses

The day trip to Carqueville reveals a strange fact about the nature of *In Search of Lost Time*: that the endless permutations of self and perception, of memory whose detail staggers the reader's mind, the sense that the novel reveals the mind as a repository of memory, whose volumes include every lived experience, is not what the novel offers, is not what the novel is about. Throughout the novel's thousands of pages, Proust complains about the failures of his memory, often claiming that his memory is not a good one. Strangely, unexpectedly, one cannot savor the depths of his writing until one believes his complaint to be true. The three trees reveal to him, as well as to us, that a wordless abyss threatens memory's lights—that lurking in all knowledge, even self-knowledge, is a dark emptiness encircled by leaves. Be they the leaves of a tree or the leaves of a book, it does not matter. Proust can hear inside words, can hear inside music, the silence against which both create their meaning. The urgency of music is that music must end. Silence, like ivy on stone, will always reassert itself. And so in us, a seed of non-experience lurks within our experience. The *a priori* haunts the skull—not as that which occurs before all experience, but that which is included in every experience. There is something in this life we live that we cannot know. This lack of knowledge, more profoundly even than the vicissitudes of memory, is

Proust's topic. It is also why the encounter with the ivy-clad church and the three trees is a prelude to meeting the gang of beautiful girls in Balbec, that group that includes Albertine, with whom Proust will fall into, and fall out of, his tortured love.

Love requires the paradoxical ability to recognize in another what you do not know about them. Love introduces us to absence. Love initiates us into mystery. Love is difficult because, as Proust did with the three trees, we often fill in our own voices for those voices we cannot hear, those others we do not know. The threat a lover presents to the beloved is making of her another version of ourselves—of voicing her thoughts as her own, when in truth, we are using her to speak to, or of, ourselves. When Proust first sees the girls he cannot tell them apart. They seem one nebulous, multieyed, multivisaged, multilimbed mass. They maintain en masse their separation from him. He is not close enough to think *in* them, but only *of* them. He watches as an old banker settles into a deck chair abutting the bandstand: "The floor of the bandstand jutted out above the old man's head, forming a natural springboard so tempting that the eldest of the little gang of girls, without the slightest hesitation, dashed across and jumped off the edge, sailing right over him; he was terrified by a pair of nimble feet grazing his nautical cap. . . ." The gang of girls, the eldest in particular, merge into a figure of Eros, as in Plato's *Symposium,* the god that steps on the heads of humans to walk. Just as, in his childhood bedroom in Combray, the young narrator went to bed watching the zoetrope cast spinning images of fairy tales on the walls, so now enchantment occurs before experience. Proust is aware of how the mythic, the wonderful, exerts a pressure on the mind that habituates it to its later thinking. Reality begins in this introduction to illusion. And so the gang of girls is not simply a gang of girls, but a multibodied manifestation of the god of Love. They are a cloudlike Eros; they are Eros in the cloud. And, as with anything of true wonderment, Proust cannot take his eyes, nor turn his mind, away.

Among the more famous moments in Proust—the madeleine dipped in Aunt Leonie's lemon tea, the cobblestones, the childhood book found in the library—there is one sentence I return to more than any other. The sentence feels somehow more indicative of the hidden work *In Search of Lost Time* enacts—not the wondrous removal of time through repetition in time, but this other work that occurs in a life devoted to the intricate combination of love and thought: the work of arrival in what one cannot know, the work of being present without knowing; that is, the work of wonder. Before Proust knows any of the little gang of girls, but after he knows he is in love with them, he sees them, and in thinking of them, thinks himself toward them:

> For this present object was the one I would have preferred above all, as I knew perfectly well, having botanized so much among young blossoms, that it would be impossible to come upon a bouquet of rarer varieties than these buds, which, as I looked at them now, decorated the line of the water with their gentle stems, like a gardenful of Carolina roses edging a cliff top, where a whole stretch of ocean can fit between adjacent flowers, and a steamer is so slow to cover the flat blue line separating two stalks that an idling butterfly can loiter on a bloom that the ship's hull has long since passed, and is so sure of being first to reach the next flower that it can delay its departure until the moment when, between the vessel's bow and the nearest petal of the

one toward which it is sailing, nothing remains but
a tiny gap glowing blue.

As with the three trees, the girls confront Proust with an entity that
confounds his intelligence. But unlike the experience with the trees in
which he fills in their silence with his own voice, Proust reacts to his
vision differently. The sentence begins in euphemism, a sort of low-
grade metonymy by which we know that he is the "botanizer" and
the girls are "the young blossoms." There is a degree of lecherous
self-knowledge in the tone—a kind of winking of the eye behind the
words. But when the sentence reaches the simile it pivots into a different kind of vision—one more definite for being less knowing. Proust
steps away from knowledge, away from wit, and enters into vision.
Thinking disrobes and becomes sight. That vision hovers indistinctly
between the symbolic and the actual. He sees that between two roses
an entire ocean can fit. Zeno exerts as much influence on the moment
as does Heraclitus, who leaning back in the grass, noted that his toe
covered up the sun. A steamer carries its passengers slowly from—so
it seems to the eye watching it—one rose to the next. The slowness
of the ship is the result of its great distance, but the eye doesn't see in
distance—the mind does. And here, the thinking that's done requires
the mind's absence. The thinking is in the eye. A butterfly idles in
one of the roses and need not hurry to know it will reach the other
rose before the steamer does. Why should that which arrives first
be of concern? The mind knows that the ship is miles distant from
the rose from which the butterfly will sip; the eye doesn't know. The
eye sees that the steamer and the butterfly share a principle and so
are in a kind of competition. Who will arrive first? Who will feast?
Zeno holds the ship in its infinitesimal distance, its "tiny glowing
gap of blue." But the butterfly breaks through the infinitesimal gap;
the butterfly breaks through the last vestige of philosophy the eye

contains. The butterfly arrives, and will always arrive—at least in the vision of the sentence—before the steamer does.

As with the three trees, we know that the steamer and the butterfly represent the narrator himself. Unlike the earlier moment, this identification isn't willful but allegorical. The more metaphoric the sentence becomes, the more actual the vision seems. We forget the girls are the roses; we forget that narrator is the boat and butterfly both. We forget because the narrator himself forgets. The vision offers its own lesson, and it is a lesson about love and otherness. Should the steamer arrive before the butterfly at the rose, the rose becomes merely a port of destination, an accomplishment, a stop on an itinerary. Because the rose is a girl such a stop is a form of love and makes of the lover a kind of tourist admiring his own good taste in destination. Such a love ends in knowledge because its value is experience. The butterfly doesn't arrive at the rose, it enters into it. It doesn't profit from the rose, it doesn't learn from the rose, it lives upon it, it thrives within it, and in doing so, lets the rose live, lets the rose thrive. Such a love is a kind of living—living in such a way that the difference between petal and wing becomes ever harder to distinguish, until the butterfly's idling is done. Every rose on the rose bush is the same rose. The passenger on the steamer doesn't know this fact, though the butterfly does. When the passenger leaves it is heartless betrayal; when the butterfly leaves it is acceptance merged with hunger.

Not all lust decays the one who lusts. Lust on the hull of the steamer is slowly growing rust. Lust in the butterfly is the light coating of the stamen's dust. One lust ends in a knowledge wonder can't undo. The other ends in wonder knowledge cannot fill. What marks so deeply the narrator of *In Search of Lost Time* is the presence of both kinds of desire. When the girls transform into flowers he transforms into a boat and butterfly. His mind idles. His eye shows him both ways in which he might arrive.

III. Meditations in the Hut

I.

Let's begin with a basic claim, not as truth or fact, but as possibility: reading is a form of experience. Hands hold the book's heft; eyes read the words; the body is involved though we forget so. Reading seems something more than or less than experience, occurring, as it does, in some twofold world happening simultaneously in the author's mind and the reader's mind with only the thin printed page as conduit between. Of course, that page is no pure conduit: a word is an imperfect conductor, as given to insulating properties as to conductive ones. Somewhere in Shakespeare's language lingers the remnant heat of Shakespeare's thoughts, somewhere in those words is the blast-furnace of his genius. At times that genius burns through the page into the reader's mind, but at other times the language holds its heat, and the page seems only to warm by virtue of the living hands in which it's held. Those hands are our hands. Reading forges experience inside of experience, the book unfolds in the mind, unfolds in the imagination, not as book but as world, as life or a form of life, even as the book sits in the hands, even as it speaks into the eyes that read it. Reading, at times, is an experience that obscures experience, an experience that mars itself—when we feel we're reading successfully, that is deeply and vividly, we forget there is a book being read, we forget our hands hold the book, we see with different eyes than the eyes through which we see. It is like a dream, reading.

That word, *dream,* it invokes in me a memory of a passage that speaks to the doubtful nature of experience reading offers. The passage is from the opening of John Bunyan's *Pilgrim's Progress*:

> As I walked through the wilderness of this world,
> I lighted on a certain place where was a Den, and
> laid me down in that place to sleep: and, as I slept,
> I dreamed a dream. I dreamed, and behold, I saw a
> man clothed with rags, standing in a certain place,
> with his face from his own house, a book in his
> hand, and a great burden upon his back. I looked,
> and saw him open the book, and read therein; and,
> as he read, he wept and trembled; and, not being
> able longer to contain, he brake out with a lamentable cry, saying, "What shall I do?"

I can see certain things in this certain place in which the dreamer and the reader coexist. The reader lives within the dreamer's mind. It is an exquisite reversal: to find within the mind itself the book open in the hands. I see that the book isn't the burden, but the book is not release from that burden. Perhaps the book is the burden we choose to hold, and when we hold it, we do so always so that the book is in front of us. Perhaps the book is what makes us aware that on our backs is a burden; perhaps what the reader reads is the awful information that on our back we bear a great burden, and our comfort shifts to discomfort, our ease to difficulty, and the shock is that what we just now sense, by virtue of the book, has always been so. The burden has never not been on our backs. A book contains a world; it is a world we carry in our hands. It is a burden differently than is the back's burden. The book is the burden we read, and that is heavier than the burden we bear. The book does not give us an answer, but gives voice to our weeping and trembling. The book lets us know that we don't know what we are doing. The book doesn't bewilder us; the book gives us our bewilderment; it is a kind of gift. We read the book, and then we ask what it is *we shall do.*

2.

Some of what we do is we think. One of the curious aspects of reading is that it fills the mind with a peculiar resource. It's as if the convolutions of the brain were some sort of multidimensional library, in which Melville's "late-consumptive usher at a grammar school" pulls from shelves those books that thought itself unwittingly requests, and so brings those pages to mind. Sometimes I think the doubled I of Descartes's *I think, therefore I am* includes in the first utterance a librarian self who brings forth those texts that confirm the existence of the latter. The books says "I" before I do.

It is a strange library—thinking—where nothing arrives complete.

Often, when I think about what it means to read, what arrives in response is not a book. It is a photograph, and though what I know of the picture undoubtedly came from the explanation posted beside it, I have no memory of reading the placard. What I know of it seems written within the picture itself.

I saw this photo in the museum in which I used to work. It is of a boy who seems quite young. He is curled up so that his knees are near his chin, and resting on his knees is an open book. The boy's eyes stare haphazardly at the sky, the blank-pupil stare of the blind. The boy has no arms: he lost them to a bomb or grenade. And what the boy is doing is this: having been born blind, and having learned braille, he is bending his face down to the book so that he can read the bumps on the page with his lips.

I don't know what reading is; I know this picture says much about reading.

3.

The next unbidden thought, a thought I haven't been able to shake for many years now, is Bede's story of Caedmon and his hymn. Reading asks a question of origins, a question beneath itself. This story of the first poem written in the language in which I write poems exerts on me a mysterious pull. Caedmon, among his fellow herdsmen, feels he cannot participate in their singing; he feels that he can sing no song. He leaves the revelry and goes to the hut in which the animals are kept, and among the animals he falls asleep. He dreams a dream, and in that dream a man appears to him and asks him to sing his song. Caedmon replies that he cannot sing. The man says, "Nevertheless, you must sing. You must sing me a song of the first Creation." And Caedmon, whose mind before could not fill his mouth with words, finds in him his song. That song begins: "Now we must praise." When he wakes from his dream he remembers this song and all the songs that in his sleep he sung.

That the first song is a song of praise means much to me—that lyric impulse to recognize and attend to that which already exists, but exists newly in the poem's praise. What I like more, and take more seriously, is that such songs begin in impossibility, in not being able to sing. The beginning of poetry is in this failure, this saying that "I cannot do it," and leaving to go the hut and sleep with the animals— animals whose lives, too, are a song they cannot sing for themselves. This hut is also the hut of poetry. In that hut, when conscious failure relents to unconscious sleep, a visitor appears and commands us to readdress our failure. It is within this failure that we find our song. We cannot do it ourselves. We need a stranger to guide us. We are given our voices by others.

Books are also these visitors to us, entering into our minds where our minds are asleep, that place where reason lets down its guard and a world awakens unbidden within us. And that world also asks of us who read, and in reading, let that world occur, to sing of it and in it. And where we have no song, the book puts in us song. And that song is always a song of creation.

4.

I am not an expert on the issues I'm trying to speak about. Far more simply, I'm a practitioner—and these meditations on the ways in which reading and writing coexist as two activities so interrelated as to be aptly considered one are merely a result of that practice. My poetry life has been deeply devoted to the act of reading. At times, even at most times, writing feels to me a work that aims at reading as its most hopeful end—not a poem's *being read,* but that by the work of writing, I can more accurately turn my attention back to the inspiring text that is not my own. Emerson's suggestion in "The American Scholar," that "there is creative reading as well as creative writing," has become the primary touchstone of my creative life. What I would like to do is think about what some of the implications within a notion of "creative reading" might be—and how those implications might re-exert themselves in the work of writing. Sometimes I think that the gift of writing is that it makes reading more possible, as if written expression were somehow the sacrifice necessary to be let into the open field of another's pages, not merely as a reader of them, but a participant in them. A poem is a kind of Charon's coin: it is the price for passage. And make no doubt, as with Charon's boat, the passage we undergo, between the shore of writing and the far shore of reading, is one that also passes between life and death, that complicates the ease of that most basic of oppositions—but more on that later, when we've more properly gotten aboard the boat, more after we've paid our fare.

5.

Reading, by its nature, is a receptive activity, but for the poet, reading is miraculously a perceptive one as well. I take Keats all too seriously when he suggests that intelligences are "atoms of perception." "Intelligences" for him implies both an ideal and anonymous capacity of mind that only a "world of pains and troubles" can transmute into identity. We are alive to the degree we are woundable, and the most basic wound which offers us experience is the wound of the eye—that hole, that pupil (where the pun of the eye as a student must be present to be appreciated) which lets in light, and the world, and those words, light reveals.

But to read threatens the identity of the reader as directly as reading informs it. That is, reading adds a world to a world, adds a self to a self, and the awful pain of reading is that it takes that which is sufficient in us (self, world) and makes of it a surplus. Generosity is also a type of violence. When reading turns perceptive, when the words on the page become the world in the mind, when we realize that reading itself is an activity as rife with reality as is going for a walk or working in the garden, and in some ways is more real than those—for it includes the grammar that patterns perception, for it forces the mind into an awareness of its strategies of making of the world the reality that is the world, for it requires a consideration of the methods by which we make meaning—then we are confronted with the double vision of a world that is and is not our own.

Writing asks a question about that double world, and the double self that therein dwells. (Here I am suddenly and remarkably reminded of Thoreau standing on Walden Pond in early spring, when he sees in the meltwater on the ice a reflection of himself with another self on top of him.) We perceive through pages well read another world; it does not exactly belong to us, but it belongs to no other. Should that world simply tumble into the head, simply become an image, then reading ceases to be a creative activity and becomes merely an imaginative one. But writing takes advantage of this excess of self, this excess of world, which reading offers. Writing becomes the creative means of approaching such a world, of entering into it, and in so doing, positing its reality as a kind of destination—a place in which thought and experience occur within one another, though the reality of it isn't simply tangible. Writing into that space of reading reifies a world that otherwise would be lost—it sustains, it is a form of sustenance.

6.

When Hermes—god of language and lyric, god of gambling and lying—is but a day old, he leaves his mother's cavern and crawls outside. He sees a tortoise and says (in Lewis Hyde's translation): "If you were to die you'd sing most beautifully." He then invites the animal in, scoops out its insides with a silver spoon, and creates from its shell the lyre. As with Caedmon, here is a tale whose power is in providing an archetype for lyric song. It is by playing this same instrument, whose notes are accompanied by infant Hermes's singing, that Hermes soothes Apollo's anger at the theft of the sun god's sacred cattle.

This tale is much shortened here, and there is much in what's left out that could also pertain to our concern, but what interests me most is the song that Hermes sings—the first lyric poem that bends the sun god from his fury. The song that Hermes sings is a theogony: a song that recounts how the world formed, the lineage of the gods that filled that world, how chaos became cosmos. What strikes me most deeply about this song isn't simply how it simultaneously recognizes Apollo and places Apollo in his proper sphere (and so the lyric poem is a form of recognition), nor how Hermes cunningly includes himself in his song and so joins the ranks of the immortal gods (and so lyric poetry is also a form of trickery and inclusion); what strikes me most deeply is that the song sings of what it cannot know.

As with Caedmon, in Hermes we find a singer whose song possesses a knowledge the singer himself cannot contain. The song contains experience the singer himself has not lived; the song itself is the experience. It sounds like a riddle, but it is no riddle, to realize that song gives us the experience we live only after having sung the song. The song posits the world the singer lives in, regardless of the impossibility that the singer must first live outside of that world, existing in some nowhere or some nothing language cannot express. The song gives us experience our own lives' limits deny us, disrupts the limit between the *a priori* and *a posteriori,* transforms the unlived into the lived, and shows how world follows from word. There is a way in which we must live inside the song to live inside the world.

7.

I'm not sure to what degree the following thoughts have taken us to any closer scrutiny of what reading is to a certain kind of writer, or more generally, and more importantly, what the complex relationship is that interfuses the work of reading with the work of writing and vice versa. There is another story that comes to mind that, I hope, can begin to braid together these loose strands of thought. The story is Middle Eastern, and is found in Daniel Heller-Roazen's *Echolalias.*

> Abu Nuwas asked Khalaf for permission to compose poetry, and Khalaf said: "I refuse to let you make a poem until you memorize a thousand pages of ancient poetry, including chants, odes, and occasional lines." So Abu Nuwas disappeared; and after a good long while, he came back and said, "I've done it."
>
> "Recite them," said Khalaf.
>
> So, Abu Nuwas began, and got through the bulk of the verses over a period of several days. Then he asked again for permission to compose poetry. Said Khalaf, "I refuse, unless you forget all one thousand lines as completely as if you had never learned them."
>
> "That's too difficult," said Abu Nuwas. "I've memorized them quite thoroughly!"

"I refuse to let you compose until you forget them," said Khalaf.

So Abu Nuwas disappeared into a monastery and remained in solitude for a period of time until he forgot the lines. He went back to Khalaf and said, "I've forgotten them so thoroughly it's as if I never memorized anything at all."

Khalaf then said, "Now go compose!"

As with Caedmon's "Hymn" and Hermes's lyric *Theogony,* I find in this anecdote some expression of the mystery I feel when I'm involved in the work of poetry. I say "work of poetry" because, as is perhaps becoming clear, I feel unable to cipher out the work of reading from the work of writing, and so seek out places in which that strange complexity can be half-lit, brought into some sort of expression, some form of thought.

Here, reading precedes the ability to write. One can guess that to memorize those thousand pages of poetry, those epics and those treatises and those occasional lines, is to both teach the issues of prosody as well as to build a resource of what's been written. That reading here is a resource is unquestionable—it is the kind of work, memorization, that forges in the mind the paths by which it will think, and what it will think of; these poems are the works that carve in the mind the ability to think in the first place. The work of memorization here is so intense as to preclude any other activity—for those years, Abu Nuwas did nothing but memorize what he read, to the exclusion of any other world than the world of the page.

Where the tale grows remarkable is that this feat, the marvel of this poetic feat, is only half the work—and the next half, before one can begin to compose verse, is to forget all that is memorized. It seems that whatever the poetic mind is, it is one in which fullness must be transformed into emptiness. That, of course, is a recipe for desire. The mind sated on pages, rife with poems, must lose every page and every poem in order to be subject to that desire which on seeing an empty page wants to fill it with song. We must be full before we are empty: full of words not our own before we can suffer the emptiness of needing our own words. It may be true that this desire for our own words is more profoundly a desire for those words that were once ours but never our own, those words others gave us. I am reminded of the fact that there is no private language, that linguistic fate is to think of myself in a language that can never be "my own." The first motion— reading—denies the self; the second motion—forgetting—reveals the self. But that self isn't in surplus, but in absence. That self is one who desires a world in words.

But there is another lesson here, more intimate to our topic. I have found it curious for some time now that the Greek root for forgetting, -lethe, rhymes with, and so shares some bond with, the root for truth, -alethe. Hidden within this discovery is the same realization: the truth contains within it its own disappearance.

One of the differences between a scholar's relationship to text and a poet's relationship to the same is that where the scholar wishes to remember, and must do so, the poet reads to remember and to forget, and must do so. We shouldn't assume that reading is learning—at least not in any normal sense. Reading is discovering truth, or what feels in text like truth, so that truth can return to nothing.

8.

I have a little daughter, just four years old, and when I put her to sleep at night I read her a book. Most parents, I'm sure, repeat the same ritual every night. Every night before I go to sleep, I read. This moment of reading before sleep has been for me, almost for as long as I can remember, one of the great pleasures of my life. I want my daughter to have the same pleasure.

But I never thought about the nature of that pleasure, about the necessity of reading before sleep. My daughter, as with many children, did not, and still does not, like going to sleep. Her mother or I need to stay in the darkened room, after the books are closed, after the stories are done, and sing songs until she drifts off to sleep. I wonder why a child fears sleep, resists it so fully, with such effort. I suppose it might be because sleep is a little deathlike, and when the world disappears, before dreams fill in and destroy the blank they also must exist within, there is no guarantee the world will exist, nor the self that thinks about the world it also must exist within, when the eyes open once again.

A book prepares a child for sleep because, like sleep, it is also a little deathlike, a little death. In the midst of the waking world the book gives the child another world, a dream within the world that slowly becomes more real than the world itself. That book-born dream seems to say to the child: don't worry, if what is here now ceases to be here in sleep, you'll still have this world I'm granting you. The blank space below the words on the page are also a kind of sleep, a kind of death, and it is only against that blankness that the words can be read. A child's book goes to great lengths to deny that blank. Pictures cover the page from margin to margin. But even in the child's book, the words must find a blank space in order to be read. Those words give the child a world more profound than do the pictures— and it is the echo of those words that not only allow a child to fall asleep, but secretly instruct her how to do so. The book begins sleep's work as sleep begins death's work. This sleep does not deny the world but lets the world go, trusts that in abyss another world will appear, reminiscent of the waking one, but altered, a world in which every figure is born from the self dreaming, a dream that in turn makes the dreamer into a self. I like to think the eye closes as do the covers of a book. The world is gone, but the words that speak the world exist still, even if unreadable, in the darkness.

9.

I have often thought of poetry as the work one must do alone that no one can do alone. The gift of the book, and the work of reading, encompass that paradox, and make of its convolutions a simpler thought. I mentioned the phrase "the hut of poetry" to make a claim about the space in which Caedmon slept and dreamt among the warm animals, but now I'd like to think more distinctly about the phrase, about the possibility that reading a poem isn't a mental activity so much as it is an elemental one. To read is to seek entrance, and fluency in a language isn't a mark of intelligence so much as it is knowing how to wield a key. A poem is remarkably a door that is also a dwelling, a plank that is also a hut. Knock your mind against it in the right way and the line opens. To be let in also predicts one's fate; that fate is to be kicked out. For Emerson is right, a poem's value is vehicular—but we should not forget that we can dwell too inside a motion. A poem is that dwelling-in-motion. Inside it we suffer meaning. That suffering, as I've tried to suggest, is not death exactly, but is death inexactly. It is also a form of wonder.

Ancient initiation rites almost invariably mimicked, as part of their ordeal, the death of the initiate. The initiate would be brought to a hut. Sometimes the door of the hut was considered the mouth of a monster, and the initiate, after undergoing what ordeals he must— being wrapped in dark shrouds, having teeth knocked out, incisions in genitalia or scarification of limbs, and so on—would be pushed out through a hole in the back of the hut, as if the monster had digested him. The idea is that the initiate lives in a sacred world but cannot recognize its sacredness. The end of initiation, and the death initiation symbolizes, is to be reborn, to have new eyes, so as to see the world as if for the first time. That is a whole and holy vision. I would like to suggest that poetry offers us just such an initiation, and the process of reading is an initiatory ordeal, and the result of that reading is the world seen through renewed eyes.

That word, "eyes," it brings me back to the blind boy missing arms but holding a book propped up on his knees. It does not feel true or right to say that reading the book with his lips will allow him to see, nor that reading will give him a world to grasp despite his having no arms, no hands. Such notions seem like a hollow comfort. But what I would like to think is that reading, and the world that fills his head when reading, doesn't undo his injury but makes his injuries meaningful. I'm still not saying it right. I mean to say his injuries become his means for making the world. Reading doesn't deny injury, nor heal it, but makes injury of use.

I have a little wound in my eye, and the light comes in. The page is a reminder of that wound. What reading gives us is a miraculous forgetting, and the end of that miracle is the world that appears in the wound.

FOUR TALES

The Song Inside the Bird Song

The boy thought there lived a child in the sun and stared up into the sun until the child could be seen: a baby swaddled in blue, curled up and sleeping in the sun's arms. The sun has no arms. The sun is a circle and embraces itself. The child stared and stared. When he turned his eyes away he still saw the sun. It hovered in front of everything else. Everywhere he looked there was the baby cradled in the sun's arms.

The boy took to sitting on his stool for many hours watching the baby. The baby always slept. It never sang. The baby lived in the boy's eyes. When the boy saw the baby he smiled. The boy smiled for hours sitting on his little stool in his room.

The boy's parents painted the walls of his room. They worried about their little boy who stared and smiled. They thought he smiled at the way the sun fell against the wall, the way the sun sparked out between the leaves, between the shadows of the leaves on the wall. His parents painted a tree on one wall. The canopy filled the wall, so that the room seemed a nest within the tree. They painted birds: yellow warblers with fire on their chests, rose-breasted grosbeaks, and shy night herons. They painted green leaves whose undersides were silver, and on the wall the wind had blown some of the leaves over, and the sun caught the silver which said rain was soon to come. Rain was soon to come. There was a window in the middle of the tree, and in the window were the dark clouds. Other days the window was bright. Then the sky was open in the tree. On another wall the boy's parents painted the ocean. They painted the ocean so the ocean extended back to the horizon where sky and sea met seamlessly. They painted rocks rising up from the floor, and the crashing waves cast up drops, and they painted those drops on the wall. There are rainbows in the mist. They painted ocean birds: white pelicans in sea and in sky, their white wings flashing in sunlight as they fly, arctic terns, and on the rocks sandpipers on their yellow legs. There was a light where the sea met the sky his parents turned on and dimmed at night. His parents painted a meadow on a wall. The meadow was ringed by pines. The tall grass bent down when the head grew heavy with seeds. Wind pushed the grass into a pattern. Where deer slept the grass was matted down. There were flowers in the meadow: the wild carrot whose white lace blossom had in its center a single purple petal. Ants crawled up the stems; the stems of some flowers were finely haired. There were bees in the field, bees deep in the flowers in the field, the pollen heavy on their legs, heavy on the legs of the bees in the flowers in the field. The meadow rose up and touched the ceiling. There were birds in the meadow: bobolinks with the yellow sun behind their heads, yellow-headed blackbirds whose head was a sun, the meadowlark who wore the sun on his chest. In the middle of the meadow a mirror hung so the boy could see himself looking at the meadow. His parents painted the sky on a wall. The sky was darker as it rose, with a single star, the morning star, placed in the darkness. The middle of the sky was bright and filled with clouds. None of them built darkly into thunderheads. These clouds were gentle clouds. The boy could see animal shapes in the clouds if he looked long enough. That cloud was almost a rabbit; that cloud was almost a mouse. That cloud was the lion's mane but the lion had escaped from the sky. His parents painted birds in the sky: blue heron with his neck curled into an *s* as he flew, common goldeneyes flying in their *v,* and swallows, swallows, who once hatched, never touch the ground. The lower sky was pale yellow as if the sun were rising. This wall was a day. There was a row of hooks nailed to the sky where the boy could hang his jacket.

His parents worried about him, their little boy who sat and smiled, who never misbehaved, who was docile and kind, who seemed to live in his own world in which they didn't know if they too lived, and so they painted his room. They painted the world on the walls of his room. But when the boy looked at the walls, when he stood inside the tree, when he stood in the meadow, when he stood by the sea, when he stood in the blue cloudy sky, he saw everything through the face of the baby cradled in the circle of the sun, and he smiled.

. . .

His parents met in a little town when the man who was his father traveled through. The woman who was his mother sat in the garden painting watercolors of bees in irises. She sang softly to herself as she worked, and the man stopped and listened. He stayed many days. They would walk, in the late summer evenings, when the day extended out through time, to the meadow beyond the town. A trail led through the woods, and when the woods ended, the trail opened into a meadow that sloped gently down to the sea. The man didn't know they were so near the coast and the woman laughed. They would lie down in the meadow and watch the sky and the clouds filling the sky and the birds flying below the clouds.

After they married, after the young woman had left the town, after they had settled in the city where they now live, they would try to go back to the meadow, but could never find it. They could not find the woods, they could not find the meadow, they could not find the ocean or the sky. They could not find the little town the woman was from, and this caused her much grief. Where was the garden with the bees in the irises? Where was the song she sang in the garden?

The boy's parents painted his walls from their memory of the place in which they had talked and fallen in love. The boy became possible in that field. He was for them the field's embodiment: tree growing up from shoulders, body as fragrant field, eyes as sky above mouth as ocean. They had in him what they lost in the world. But when their boy ceased to speak, when moods stopped flashing like weather across his face, when he sat on his stool and smiled, his parents felt as if they'd lost the place again; that the field had retreated, the woods and the sky and the sea had retreated deep into their little boy, in a recess forged by deep silence, by simple faith, a chamber in the heart, perhaps, or a chamber behind the eye; their child began to escape into himself just as the meadow escaped into itself, just as the woods and the sky and the sea escaped into themselves, and his parents began to fear that soon they'd have only the charcoal portrait the woman had drawn of their son sitting and smiling on his stool to remember him by. The portrait hung in an oval frame in the hallway. In it his eyes were closed.

. . .

The parents decided to take their boy on a trip. They thought that a change of location, leaving his room with the painted walls, leaving his little stool, might waken him out of his reverie. They packed clothes and packed food and packed the tent in the car. The boy sat in the back seat looking out the window. His parents thought the quality of his smile had changed, had become more thoughtful, more aware or attentive, but it hadn't. The boy saw the baby on the side of the road, hovering above the weeds, keeping pace with the car. The boy saw his own face reflected in the window he stared out of, so that his own face hovered in front of the baby's face hovering in front of the world. His parents talked amongst themselves. They'd grown so used to the boy's silence that they forgot he might be listening. They spoke of their own parents. The boy's mother cried. The boy's father came to the grim conclusion that everything we love we lose and he said so. Then his parents were silent. Then his mother stared out her window as the boy stared out his own. And the father drove.

At lunchtime they pulled the car off the road. They found a picnic table by a river. Across the river were dark woods. The noise of the highway and the sound of the river were a song in counterpoint. They found in the weeds and grass the typical highway detritus. The mother picked up a receipt for charcoal briquettes and relish and birdseed that, according to the date printed on it, was twelve years old. "Look," she said to her boy, "this page is older than you." The boy smiled. The baby hovered over his mother's face and seemed to say to the boy, "Look, this page is older than you."

His parents spread out a blanket. They didn't want to sit at the picnic table which was in disrepair and inscribed all over with declarations of love and curses against those in love. They spread out their red blanket near the river and laid out the food they'd brought: sandwiches, orange slices, popcorn, and lemonade.

While his parents prepared lunch the boy stood by the river looking at the woods across it. The baby's face had grown larger in his eyes. All the woods were within the baby's face, and when the baby opened its mouth birdsong sang out. The boy thought the baby was speaking to him, asking him to come into the woods.

When his parents called for him the boy was gone. His father ran to the river and saw, walking across the field toward the woods, his boy. "Come quickly," he yelled to his wife, who ran over, breathless in panic. The river was deep and swift from the spring melt. How could our boy have crossed it? they thought, as the father slowly made his way across the current, his wife holding on to him as he went. The boy was entering the woods as his parents stepped up the river's bank. They watched him as he disappeared. The mother thought, but did not say, I knew it would happen. I knew it would be this way. The father did not think at all, just grabbed his wife hand's and, keeping his eye on the spot where his boy walked into the woods—between two black cherry trees whose joining boughs seemed to form an arch—hurried through the field. Where the boy had walked the grass was tamped down. Out of the corner of her eye his mother saw a fly land on a sprig of wild parsley. His father saw a cloud's shadow pass over the milkweed and bindweed. But when they reached the edge of the woods, when they stood under the bower of the black cherry trees, their boy was gone. The forest floor kept no prints.

The father was desperate but the mother thought, We must quiet our despair. She held her husband's hand and said, "Shh, Shh, Shh," over and over again. And when they were both quiet they heard, not footsteps, not a voice, but a birdsong ringing out clearly among the other sounds of the woods. It was a little ovenbird singing "teacher, teacher." The parents stepped toward the song, and as they walked toward it, the song stepped back, singing again clearly to them. So they moved through the woods as if in a dream. The parents did not know how long they followed the ovenbird's song. The light in the woods never changed but it felt as if days had passed. The mother still had the receipt crumpled up in her hand but, when she looked down at it, the ink was smudged, as if erased, almost blank. When she looked up the song ceased singing. They stood on the edge, the opposite edge, of the woods the bird had guided them through. Below them a meadow sloped gently down. In the meadow, where the deer had slept, the grass and the flowers were bent down. A bee stood on a thistle. The touch-me-not fell apart at a touch. A beetle crawled across the dirt, leaving in the fine dust a script behind it. The parents walked through the meadow. They didn't see their boy but their panic had been replaced by a calm filled with expectation. The sky was blue and the clouds in it white and the birds flying in the sky below the clouds looked gray and black or, suddenly caught in the sun, a brilliant flashing white that made the clouds seem suddenly strangely dull. They felt they had found something or been found by something. They kept walking. They heard the sea crashing against the rocks before they saw the sea crashing against the rocks. Where the meadow ended the ocean began. An arctic tern gazed at them with its head cocked and then flew away. His father thought the tern might fly around the world. His mother thought the tern would dive into the ocean and sleep on the waves.

It was when they turned their heads back toward the meadow, the golden meadow crowned by the dark woods, that they saw him, their son. Their hearts didn't leap but beat steadier. There was their boy, back turned to them, looking up at the sky and gently rocking back and forth. His parents walked to him. They didn't call out his name. They didn't hurry. There was no rush. They walked toward him through the field where long ago they fell in love. And when they reached him, he seemed not to notice they were there, standing so close behind him. His father almost said his boy's name but stopped himself. His mother almost reached out her hand to touch his shoulder but stopped herself. The boy stood and gently rocked, looking up at the sky. Time passed, but time had ceased to measure the progress of the day. Time measured something else, some nameless thing. And when the boy did turn around, his eyes were open and he was smiling. He looked at them and saw them. His parents could feel in his gaze that he saw them. The baby had left his eyes where it had been living. He held in his arms a bundle wrapped in blue cloth. He smiled and smiled and his parents smiled back. His mother began to cry. His father's hand was shaking slightly. The boy looked down at the bundle in his arms, the blue-wrapped bundle, and looking back up at his parents, he smiled, he smiled and opened his mouth, he looked around him at the meadow, he looked down to the sea and up the woods, and he said, as he held out his arms, "Here it is."

The Children, the Woods

Clouds veiled the face of the blue moon the night the twins were born. One child was the moon, and one the cloud half-lit by moon. The boy's eyes were dark as were his mother's. His sister's eyes were pale as moonlight on leaves. No one in the family had eyes like hers, save the rumors of their great-great-grandmother's sister who, according to the tales the boy grew up hearing, was a witch, and who, in her yellowing daguerreotype on the wall, taken in bright sunlight, seemed to have no eyes at all. Father told him stories that he had been told as a child. The dust on the floor of her house would sweep into ciphers behind her when she walked through a room, spelling out the fate of her visitor. Her left hand cold, her right hand hot. A flower in her left hand would look perfectly preserved, but crumble at the slightest touch; a flower in her right hand would wilt, leaves and petals sear at their edges. Men traveled great distances to learn from her their fortune. One man held out his palm to her, and the line that divided his palm in two filled with a trickle of blood as she traced her nail along it. The man cried and ran out the door, but returned that night with others, stones in hand, to force her from her home. Father told the boy these stories before leaving to work at the forge behind the house, the sound of the hammer on metal a punctuation to the boy's fear as he cleaned up and did his chores.

Every night the father would tell the boy the same story before bed. Sitting on the edge of the bed, the firelight a dim glow through the bedroom door, the smell of metal on his blackened hands, he'd begin. *Once upon a time, two weeks after the blue moon, when the old moon held the new moon in her arms, a man with no face walked into the house where twins—a boy and a girl—had just been born. If the stranger had a face, it couldn't be seen. A black veil hung before it, a cloth dark and fine as night held darkly between branches in the woods, a night darker than the night above, and behind the veil, as the moon behind dark clouds, a dim glow. The stranger walked over to the mother and closed her eyes with his hand. Then he bent down, took the baby girl from the cradle, put her inside his coat, and holding her to his chest with one arm, walked out the door. Black threads marked his path through the room, the fallen remnants from the cloth covering his face. The father, stunned while the stranger stood in the room, stood up from his chair, grabbed a lantern, and ran to the door. The yellow lantern light revealed a darkly marked path through the lawn to the edge of the woods, like crape unrolled, dividing the grass in two.* To the boy's questions the father would answer, *She became a child of woods. There are many such children. People say they hear them whisper and play in the night. The mother never opened her eyes again, nor could she, until the baby boy grew up, entered the forest, and returned with his sister that the stranger stole. Why did the stranger steal the girl? Because, she was the moon's child, and the night wanted her return.* This was the story his father told him every night. Then he would gently push the metal cylinder, chased with holes, which spun around the candle flame. The light through the metal cast the shape of a baby crawling on the wall, and following the baby, a child walking, and following the child, a wolf running, and following the wolf, the baby came crawling once more. The father made the toy himself to help his boy fall asleep. First the wolf hunted the baby, and then the baby chased the wolf.

. . .

The boy stopped talking when the blue moon returned. His father thought the boy a simpleton. He brought the boy to the forge to watch him work, considering school a waste of the boy's time. Better to keep him close to the house, to do what chores he could manage to do, and to learn to hit metal with a hammer, or to help those who do such work, if he could not learn the art. The boy watched the orange light swallow his father as he plunged the metal into the flame, watched the white glow of the hot metal against the anvil, watched the sparks spring up with every blow of the hammer, a universe born from nothing and to nothing fading back at every strike, and then the steam heat shrouds itself in when the metal tempered cool in the vat of water. The boy would listen to his father mutter strange riddles to himself. *Where is the heat in the fire?* Sometimes, as he worked, he would tell the boy stories about his mother. The boy listened and cried. His tears in the furnace light looked like thin rivulets of molten steel streaming down his face, and his father would walk over, take the tears in his hand, walk back to the anvil, and hammer them into two thin splinters of metal. *To remember our other life,* he would say, handing them back to the boy. This was the father's trick to stop his son's sniveling. The boy had a box in his bedroom filled with tears.

At dinner the boy watched the darkness gather in the woods. Night arrived earlier in the forest than in the world. The boy knew that night didn't fall on the forest, but rose from the woods into the sky. He saw the secret as it unfolded; he heard the darker voices that in the woods sang the darkness up into the sky. He knew the sun was only a spark cast from a hammer blow, coursing its yellow arc for a day, lighting what lay below it, darkening as it cools. The boy knew the real world was dark. The boy was so quiet he could hear the bellows inside the trees. The boy could hear the single clang of metal against metal that spun the world in a circle for another day. *What do you see?* his father would ask. *Why won't you tell me what you see?*

Silence isn't nothing, but sounds like nothing. The eyes behind silence make silence quieter, almost haunted. The boy's eyes were the colors of his mother's. She stared out at her husband through her son's silence, accusing him, so the father felt, of some misdeed he felt the guilt of, without knowing what he had done. The father began to feel that when he spoke to the boy, he spoke to them both, as if the mother had hidden herself away in her son, just as her son had once hidden inside of her.

The older the boy grew, the more his silence oppressed his father— a silence that hid larger silence within it. Silence is never singular. The boy was an absence with an absence inside him, an emptiness behind the eyes, and the father began to fear him and could not bear it.

. . .

When the boy turned twelve his father told him to leave. He feared he would harm him. He told the boy at evening. He spoke calmly, looking at the floor, the woods dark in the window behind his head, a silhouette in reverse.

The father had been dreaming dreams. Knocking the boy's teeth out with the peen of the hammer. Worse dreams. Cutting off the boy's arms. Cutting off the boy's legs. Removing his bones to count them and see if all were there. Unable to put the boy together. Hiding the boy in the fire. The boy speaking from the fire, speaking in his mother's voice, *Why? Why?* Worse dreams. Cutting off the boy's head to look for the empty chamber inside it, a doorway to another world, a world where no one was lost, where his son talked, where his wife taught his daughter to spin and weave. Voices at night told him it was true. *Look in his throat,* the voices said. *Another world is lodged in his throat, that's why the boy doesn't speak. If he says a word the world will come loose. He won't share it with you. He wants the world for himself.* The father could not tell his son about his dreams, about these voices. He only told him to leave. To not look at him. But the boy did look at him, and the father stood up from his chair and stepping quickly toward him, put his hands on either side of the boy's head, peering into his eyes, turning his head to the side, saying, *Speak, just speak,* pressing his head tighter so that burning lines coursed through the boy's skull, turning the boy's head to the side, as if looking for an angle to see behind his eyes, and finding no glimpse, taking his hands slowly away, dropping them to his side, turning around, and walking out the door. The boy could, for a long time, feel the pressure of his father's hands on his head, pulsing indentations that, as the minutes passed, grew less severe, until he felt nothing, and his father faded too, like the marks of his fingers on his son's skin, into absence.

The day was dusk. The boy ate no food, nor did he take any with him. He packed no clothes. The boy walked out the door of his home, across the yard, to the woods. The leaves a darker variation of the dark air. Whispers at the boundary. Voices the boy had always heard but never understood. Now the voices cohered, gained some shape that sounded like sense. The woods have an edge until you step into them, and then the edge is gone. The boy stood at the edge a long time, listening. There is no end to the woods. *Where my sister lives,* the boy thought, *those that enter never return.*

. . .

The boy walked through the forest all night. Night in the forest ceased to be time; night was a place. Flowers of incandescent bloom glowed faintly at the base of some trees, giving light enough to see the path he walked on. His fear threatened his silence. He imagined his silence as an expanding sphere around him, within which he walked, and the silence protected him from all that would enter it and harm him. He muted the forest he walked mute within, deafened the deafening songs of birds, the leaf blades honed against the blades of other leaves, deafened the howling wolves. When silence wasn't silent enough, the boy closed his eyes, walking blindly through the woods. He stopped when he stepped against some solid thing he could not find the end of. He stood silent, blind. He imagined his muscles turning into the bones they were stitched by sinews to. He imagined a stone in his stomach. He saw the bellows of his lungs deflate. And then, he filled his heart with leaves and moss until it did not beat. Then he was safe. Then he was the darkest thing in the dark, and he stood there, motionless, through the night.

The boy didn't know if he slept. Thoughts passed, not hours; thoughts that blurred their own edges into dreams. *I must eat,* he thought, and then thought of mushrooms, thought of mushrooms springing from the moist ground, thought of bending down to pick them, thought of poison, and saw brown spores drop in clouds from the mushroom's cap, coat his hands, and from his hand, as he watched, another forest sprang, night dark in the branches, mushrooms abundant beneath the canopy, the whole wilderness in the palm of his hand, fed by an underground spring. *I must find shelter,* he thought, and thought about his eye in its socket, a cloud in a cave. He thought of the flowers and saw the heads of children tied to strings, faces following the sun, heliotropic. The forest kept withdrawing into edges that didn't exist. A woman walked from the edge, clothed in thorns, singing a song to herself that, like honey in a broken bowl, flowed slowly out of its own form. The boy wanted to walk toward the song, the words a shadow cast upward by the melody, speaking his own silent life for him. He wanted to walk toward the song, but the song walked toward him, nearing him. Her breath was in the tune. The boy could feel her song breathe against him; to breathe was to inhale her breath, an air which entered him not as sound but as light, glowing behind his eyes, so that, should he open his eyes in the dark night, light would be thrown from them onto what he saw, the woman clothed in thorns, her eyes closed, standing within the astonishment of her own song, caught in the beams of the boy's attention. It was this light that broke, like a tendril through stone, in him as he stood, undoing his desire to be safe, to be still. Listening, he heard, it seemed to him, his own words sung from another's mouth, the unspoken words, the worries he tamped down into silence, the thick melody of each loss that led him to these woods, and an octave above, the single voice doubling itself into its own harmony, brighter notes tracing the same melodic contour through the air, resolving the mournful notes with hope culled from their own darker music. The boy opened his mouth and eyes at the same time. Light entered his eyes; light did not beam out from them. Nor did he speak to the woman. There was no woman to speak to. The night had passed. Looking up he saw the canopy of the tree he stood beneath, the leaves of a strange, slightly opaque milkiness, spreading the light into a porcelain dome above the boy's head, interlaced with darker branches that coursed jaggedly through the illuminated leaves, looking like a quickly brushed script, or like the patterns of nerves in anatomical displays of the mind. The boy looked silently up and thought. He had no choice, he realized, but to wander.

The boy walked over roots and branches, through the thick, thorny brush laden with unripe berries, through the scented air dropped from the trees. There were no paths, only openings in the undergrowth of less resistance. The boy didn't know in what direction he walked; he didn't know if, in the forest, any directions existed. The woods denied geometry's rule. The boy felt that he could spend a day walking in a circle, and arrive in a location, as night neared, that he had never crossed before. The boy walked, silent. He heard no more songs. Thinking back on his night, he realized the woman dressed in thorns was some siren vision in his dreams, as from the storybooks he paged through, singing to lure men deeper into the danger they were already in. He thought the woman who sang lived in the forest in his mind. The leaves on the trees in the forest imperfectly mirrored the light falling on them, shifting the angle, so that the boy could never gauge the time. It could be morning or it could be near night. Only his hunger and thirst marked the passing of time, increasing as the labyrinthine day progressed. Day gathered its light around him. Beyond the random path he wandered through the woods, the trees darkened, as if the night had never fully left the forest, and the sunlit day was for his benefit alone, and the true denizens of the woods made their home in darkness. Light and the boy were both strangers in the woods. Shadows lurked in the shadows. The quick periphery of his eye thought it saw, as he walked, the dark brush shift, as if a creature moved by it, or through it, though silently, more silent than the boy himself, who heard his own footsteps as they fell. It kept pace with his own pace, kept the boy in its eyes, though it, whatever it was, kept itself hidden from the boy.

The thick foliage began to clear, and the boy could see, through the gradually thinning thicket of leaves, a pond. He edged toward it warily, fearing the open space would leave him vulnerable to the dangers of the woods. But his thirst led him out. He walked to the edge of the pond. Not only could the boy see the stones and fish and pondweed that slanted away from the pond's bank, the water was of such a strange clarity, it seemed to magnify all it contained. The middle of the pond descended down into darkness, but emerging from the depth stood a leafless tree, the middle branches slightly swaying in the tug of a current, a hole somewhere in the ground, that sent the pond's water underground to emerge somewhere unknown in the breadthless woods. The boy bent down to drink, closing his eyes as he slaked his thirst. The water was so cold his teeth ached, and he could feel the rivulet of water course down, a cold metal line, his throat. He drank without cupping the water in his hands; he drank as an animal drinks, his mouth in the pond, his eyes watching the ripples course across the pond, the sky wavering in the water. When he could drink no more, he sat back on his haunches, breathed deeply, eyes closed. He heard something lapping water from the pond near him. Slowly, as if afraid the vision leaping into his eyes could harm him, he opened his eyes. He saw a wolf, the gray-black hair standing up along its spine, drinking greedily from the water, its sides heaving in with every breath, as if it had run a great distance and only now could rest, even if for an instant, before having to flee what it fled, or chase what it chased, once again. The boy fell backwards in fear, trying to scramble away, back up the bank, away from the wolf. The wolf raised its head, stared at the boy, dropped its muzzle back into the water, drank deeply again. The boy quivered, silent and afraid. The wolf turned, quietly regarding him. The boy felt intelligence behind its eyes, but whether or not that intelligence regarded him kindly or with menace, the boy couldn't tell.

The boy tensed his fingers around the stones on the bank, tensed his toes, preparing to rise. The wolf looked up. The boy thought the wolf could hear his muscles working beneath his skin; the boy thought the wolf could hear his desire to stand up. The boy felt as if the wolf—now looking at him, lowering its head below its shoulders—knew before the boy himself knew, what it is he would do.

When the boy began to stand, the wolf snarled. The boy began to inch backward, rising no further, stepping back with a leg, pushing back with a hand, inching away from the water. The wolf watched him, its head only inches above the ground, front legs bent, ready to leap, growling low, richly, almost musically, but a terrible music. When the boy had moved a few feet away, he began to rise. He looked like someone standing up after hours of prayer, moving with extraordinary caution, as if the return from bodiless contemplation to body hadn't yet taken hold, and the knees' joints might not work, might bend backward, or the muscles not obey the mind's lesser command, *rise,* when the heart still begged, *kneel.* The higher the boy rose, the louder the wolf growled, until, almost upright, the wolf's deep snarl amplified, resonated in the beast's throat, pulsing in intensity, growing in fury, until snapping his jaws in the air, the wolf barked once and leaped at the boy, knocking him over backwards, the boy's hands holding his body up behind him, the boy scrambling away, his throat and body terribly exposed, and the wolf circled around him, growling again, less ferocious, watching the boy as it snarled. Tears ran down the boy's cheeks, but he made no sound. He sat on the ground, his hands in his lap. He sat a long time; he sat until he cried no longer. The wolf calmed as the boy calmed, ceased its pacing, ceased its growling, sat down on its haunches, and yowled into the air, a sound drawn out for a long time, syncopated by notes almost human in sound. This frightened the boy again. In his fear he stood suddenly up, and again, the wolf leaped at him, knocked him over, circled him, mouth open and growling. The boy was horror-struck by the wolf's mouth. He tried to rise again and again the wolf knocked him over, knocked him backward. Before the boy could move away or try to stand again, the wolf pounced on him, front legs on the boy's chest, gray eyes staring into the boy's eyes, teeth bared. The boy thought the wolf would kill him, and in his fear, the boy heard a sound he had forgotten ever hearing. The boy heard himself say, *No.*

The wolf stepped away. The boy didn't stand up. The wolf turned around and began to walk away from him, toward the dark woods. The boy sat where he was, covered in mud and dust. The wolf loped a few lengths away, looked back, and growling, turned his snout back, repeatedly, toward the woods. The boy didn't move; he watched. The wolf circled back, came close. The boy could feel the wolf's breath on his face. The wolf put one paw on the boy's chest and pushed him over. The boy didn't yell, he didn't cry, he didn't speak again. Then the wolf clenched its teeth on the boy's shirt and pulled him across the stones toward the woods. The wolf kept dragging the boy until the shirt tore. Then the wolf bit the boy's arm. The teeth didn't break the skin, but pressed painfully into it. The wolf pulled on the silent boy's arms until the boy again heard himself say, *No.* The wolf let go. The boy asked, *Should I follow you?* The wolf turned around at the question, and the boy, knowing he should not stand up, followed the wolf on hands and knees. The wolf paused often, looking back, letting the boy catch up, before moving ahead again, waiting finally at the edge of the woods, and when the boy neared and looked into the forest, the night already rising beneath the leaves, night's dark veils between branches, the wolf entered into the forbidden woods, and the boy, his knees and hands already cut from crawling, followed.

. . .

The days and nights became simple. The boy didn't count them. Time was a where not a when. He was with the wolf in the forest. He did not stand up. He learned to walk on hands and feet, bent over, his toes digging into the ground with each step, should he need to leap, to attack, the small voles that were their meals. The wolf knew the pattern of the woods, knew the paths, but could not speak them. There was no map a wolf could draw. He led and the boy followed, learning not the shape of the woods, not how to locate where he was against where he had been; the boy only learned to be where he was. The wolf taught him *now*. Now was the thorn on the berry branch when the boy ate a berry. Now was the print his hand made as it made it. At night, the boy knew danger was near when the wolf slowed its loping pace and snarled, circling back toward the boy, as if to tell whatever creature or force threatened unseen in the darkness, *He is mine.* The boy knew, too, though how he knew, he couldn't say, that the wolf also, in protecting him from that which in the woods would harm him, also promised that figureless danger his protection would one day end, and the boy would be in the woods alone, able to make a safety only of himself.

The wolf did not speak because he could not speak. The boy's silence, willful for so long, changed. His silence became wild, became another sense, revealing the world rather than hushing it. His silence, like the wolf's, became expressive. He no longer grew quiet to think. His silence wasn't the chamber of his own unspoken thoughts, a room without a door. Now his silence was the door he walked through, and the room was himself. The boy liked feeling the low hanging leaves scratch against his back when he walked beneath them. The boy liked the scent of the loam he slept in, and the thin whine of the wolf's breathing, and the warmth of the wolf's back pressed against his own.

One day, shortly before dusk, the wolf took him to a clearing in the forest where the trees thinned into an edge and the grass grew long.

In the meadow stood a small home, the sunlight falling on a patch of yellow plaster that made up its walls. The boy had never seen a single dwelling in all his time in the woods. The closest thing he had to a house was the body of the wolf he slept next to. The wolf walked up to the door of the home, scratched against the wood with his paw, and the boy sat on his haunches behind him. The door didn't open for a long time. But when the sun's yellow light reddened, and the darkness began its nightly gathering in the forest, it did. The wolf entered, and the boy followed. Though the little home, seen from the outside, had no windows, and only the single door through which the wolf and the boy entered, the inside not only looked large, lit by a fire that burned in the middle of the room, but in the middle of each wall, the boy saw another door. The smoke from the fire rose through a smoke hole in the ceiling, through which Venus brightly shone against the early dark. A woman stood with her back to them both, stirring a pot in the flames. The wolf circled the fire, and when the boy, as had become his habit, silently began to follow, the woman, without turning around, suddenly spoke, *Stand up. You don't need to pretend you're a dog to be safe here. You're safe. I've been waiting a long time for you to come. I've been waiting since before you were born. So many years now since you entered the woods, living like a wolf to be with the wolf, to live. But now you are here, and you can stand up.* The boy listened and obeyed. He sat back on his legs, and slowly, feeling in his joints, for the first time, how much time must have passed since he last rose. He stood. In the firelight he examined his hands. The long nails dark with the dirt beneath them, the pawlike calluses on the palms of his hands. When the woman turned around the boy looked up. She was the oldest person the boy had ever seen, and he felt that he had seen her before. Her eyes were so pale she seemed to have no eyes at all, just two blanks pierced in their middles by a pencil point. Even in the dim light, her pupils didn't widen. She looked as if she were staring directly into the sun. She said, *Speak. You do not need to be silent here to be safe. I've been waiting a long time to speak with you. So many years. You've been quiet to hide. But you do not need to hide here. You can speak.* The boy stood a long time before her, not knowing what to say. *It's hard for me to talk. I'm not used to talking.* He felt uncomfortable looking at the woman, and so looked around the room. The wolf was hidden behind the fire. The boy asked, *Where do those doors lead?* The woman laughed. *Many who have stood where you now stand have asked me the very same question. The doors? They lead to rooms with other doors. Always a door in the middle of the wall. I once spent a lifetime wandering through the rooms. Then, one day, I opened a door and saw the field in the clearing again. Now I tend the fire and keep my back to it, so I know which door is which. And I wait for travelers to come. Like you.*

The boy looked at her and thought. After a moment, he said, *What are they looking for?*

The woman laughed abruptly, and as abruptly stopped. *Why, you know. They are all looking for the same thing. It doesn't matter, you know. It doesn't matter.* She laughed again, bending at the waist, but still talking. *It doesn't matter what you're looking for. It's all the same. All that matters is how you look for what you're looking for. I've lost count of how many are walking through the rooms of this house, searching their searches, even now, even now as we speak. They think the house is smaller than the forest, but it's not. I told them so. They think they can find their way because a house is a built thing. But no one's hands built this house. The forest? It's inside here. You laugh. But it's true. The forest is inside this house, but you can't tell, because your eyes can't see that it's true. You know. You know how it is. It's like when you close your eyes. The sky behind your eyes. You know how it is. The cloud in your mind taking shapes that walk in the daylight back out of your eyes.* The woman stopped talking. She turned around and stirred the pot, muttering softly to herself. The boy couldn't hear the words, only the music beneath the song. And with her back to him, *So tell me what you think you're looking for?*

I've come to find my sister. She was stolen by a man who took her to the woods. I need to find her, to rescue her. The boy could not grow accustomed to hearing himself speak. His voice sounded so different in the air than in his head, and as he followed the wolf through the woods, he even ceased to listen to that voice. He had the awful feeling that someone else spoke when he was speaking, and that he listened, helpless, as the words came out.

The woman turned around and stared at him a long time. *You think she needs rescuing, your sister? Your father taught you to think like that.* The boy looked at her. He opened his mouth to speak, but closed it again. *Yes, I know your father. I know he sent you away. I saw it. You look so scared but you shouldn't be scared. Come here. Come closer. Let me read your palm.*

The boy walked to her, held out his hand. *Please, don't hurt me,* he said. The old woman put her left hand beneath his hand; her hand felt cold beneath his own. Her fingertip burned against his cold palm, tracing a fiery line that split his hand in half. *I know who it is who stole your sister. A man with no face? I know that story you've been told. The man's face is covered by the night, and in these woods, his is a power none can counter. But I will tell you a secret. I'll tell you how to find him. You and I, do you know? We're kin, we're blood.* The boy trembled. Her fingertip pressed its burning point into the base of his thumb. *Do you know my story? You know part of it. You've been told. I came to these woods; they forced me from the town, the mob. I came to this house. I spent a lifetime wandering through these doors, an endless circuit, without direction. Infinite doors to infinite rooms. Then I heard a knocking. I opened the door, and standing in the meadow was the man who took your sister. A wolf stood next* to him. *That same wolf in the room with us now. The man turned around and walked into the woods. The wolf followed. That wolf is the man's helper. He sent that wolf to find you, to help you. When the man and the wolf disappeared into the forest, I closed the door, turned my back to it so I could remember it, the only door that leads back out to the world, and began to tend this fire, to stir this pot, and wait for those who come.*

She let go of the boy's hand. *Tell me what to do,* he said.

The woman reached into a pocket in her dress, and pulled out a knife. *You must take this knife and kill and skin the wolf.* Then she reached into another pocket, and pulled out a needle and thread. *Then you must sew yourself into the wolf's skin. I'll open the door to the woods. Then you must go. You cannot follow the wolf to his master. The wolf can only go alone.*

The boy felt nauseous, felt weak, when he took the knife in his hand. He walked around the fire to where the wolf slept. He heard the woman muttering in her singsong voice behind him, stirring her pot. The boy ran his hand down the wolf's spine. *I can't do this,* he said. *The wolf protected me, taught me.* He'd never petted the wolf before. The wolf stretched out it limbs in its sleep, stretched out its neck, as if knowing what the boy must do and comforting him, forgiving him for the act not yet done. *You don't understand the woods,* the old woman said. *Why do you think the wolf taught you to walk like he walked, eat as he ate? The wolf knows, as the man who sent him knows, that you must borrow the wolf's skin, and when you're done with it, give it back. This is the kindness of the woods.* The boy grabbed the loose skin at the nape of its neck, said quietly, tearfully, *I'm sorry,* and steadying his shaking hand, he slit the wolf's throat. The woman sang and muttered behind him. The blood fell through his hands onto the floor. The boy cried. He cried as he sliced open the wolf's belly. He cried as he slid the knife between the skin and the muscle, and did the slow work of removing its hide. Time did not cease as he worked, but time did not pass. The woman never added another log to the fire, but the fire never dwindled. When the skin had been removed, the woman said, *Boy, bring the body here and throw it in the pot.* The boy lifted the wolf. He did not know it would be so light, so meager a thing. He carried the wolf over, and dropped its body in the cauldron. The fire singed the hair on his arm, a smell that filled the room. *Good,* the woman said, *good.* The boy walked back to the skin on the floor. The woman said, *You must cut off the front paws so your hands are free to sew.* The boy did so. Then he put his legs into the wolf's legs, the skin expanding as he pulled the skin on, but his leg also growing thinner, tapering at the foot, molding itself to the skin he was putting on. The boy reached back and pulled the wolf's head like a hood over his own. Then, as if he were slipping on a coat before going outside, he put his arms through the sleeves of the wolf's arms, his hands still his own where the wolfskin stopped, a gray cuff around his wrist. The boy sat on the ground, and with needle and thread, looking down at his work, sewed the belly whole from stomach to throat. And then his work was done. The boy was a wolf with human hands. The woman clapped and laughed, *You've done well.* The boy tried to thank her, but he could not speak. His tongue ran against his sharp teeth. He sat back on his haunches and yowled. He listened to the sound echo through the room. It was the first time his voice had felt like his own.

The boy walked across the room, listening to his nails scratching against the wood floor. The woman filled a bowl with the ladle with which she had been stirring the pot. The boy ate, and his hunger ceased. She pet him, running her cool hand along his spine. He went to the door. When he stood up on his hind legs, looked back at the old woman, her back was to him again. Then he turned the knob with his hand, and walked out into the clearing. It was night. There were no stars. There was no moon. The night, though, was not so dark. Seeing through the wolf's eyes he could see. He thought he saw a lupine tail disappear into the woods, the low branches shifting as the body moved through them. He thought the tail was the tail of his friend, whom he had followed for so long. Blood is a habit, coursing from heart to veins and back again. Habit, too, becomes a kind of blood. The boy thought he saw the wolf's tail disappear into the woods, and so bounding through the long grass, he followed.

. . .

The boy ran through the night. What before appeared in his eyes as darkness now he saw as limned with light, a stellar light shaken down through the atmosphere, the trembling leaves, half-lit by their own existence. The boy could see the paths the animals used. Absence left a scent. Nothing was blank. He listened to the night birds sing, each melody bodying forth the bird that voiced it. He heard the pitch of air beneath the moth's wings, the dead leaves moved by the air forced out from the hovering. He ran. His running didn't replace his thought. His running and his thinking were the same effort, the same work, indecipherable from one another. He did not think, *I'm running*. He ran. The boy didn't follow a scent, he followed the only thing in the woods he could find that did not glow dimly of its own light. Through his new eyes, his wolf eyes, the boy could see thin black threads scattered on the dead leaves on the ground, lodged like a single thistle strand on the nettle leaves, a dead-black filament clinging to the unripe berries.

When the moon rose he felt a lunar heat on his back, a tug on a vein. He did not think, *The moon is rising*.

When the sun rose he could see what in the forest refused the sunlight, and he followed it. He did not think, *It is the day*.

He did not think about time passing. He saw that his running on the earth made it spin. Night was one half of the world, and day the other. The boy followed a darker night than night, not the opposite of day, not the hemisphere's unspoken half, but a night indivisible into hours, a night never promising dawn, not measuring time, the dark that surrounded the outermost stars. He followed the night that veiled the face of the world. He followed the man who wore the veil, the man who lived inside the night. *The man who left this trail,* he thought as he ran upon the trail.

. . .

The boy did not know how long he ran. Time was not time, nor distance, distance. The path asked no questions. He ran. He endured a duration. He heard his blood pulse in his ears. He listened to the sound of his hands and feet pressing into the world. He followed the trail the night left behind.

Those dark threads led the boy to a circular hut. A pole held up a roof of interwoven leaves that sloped down to the moss-covered branches that formed the hut's walls. No door, just an opening between branches near the bottom of the wall, too small for a man to enter, but large enough for a wolf. The boy walked in.

Let your eyes adjust, a voice said. The voice didn't echo, didn't resonate. The last word ended in silence that did not end. *In here, it's dark.* The words did not light the darkness. *You've come to find me. Now you've found me. Now you must be patient. Let your eyes adjust.* The boy didn't think. He could not speak. He lay down in the dark, his palms stretched out against the cool dirt floor, rested his muzzle on his forelegs, closed his eyes, and slept.

He opened his eyes when he felt a hand running through the thick fur of his neck. Then he could see. A man with no face bent down in front of him. No eyes looked in the boy's eyes. The night was a veil hanging before the man's face, a dim glow behind. The boy looked around the hut. A pile of dark leaves on the floor. A center pole holding up the sky. *I stitch those leaves together,* the man said. His voice sounded as if spoken from a deep hollow. He spoke, so it seemed to the boy, in echo—repeating words spoken by another person in another life. Even in speaking he was silent. *You think you came here to kill me,* he said. *But I brought you here to me to help you. I sent you my wolf. The wolf you now are. The story your father told you is true. I did take your baby sister. I did put your mother to sleep. She's still asleep. Somewhere in the woods. If not these woods, another woods, another world. I don't know where.* The man stood up, and the boy stood, too. The man kept running his hand along the fur on the boy's back with a familiarity that calmed the boy, as if the nerves of the wolf in whose skin he dressed remembered the hand of his master. The man pointed to the top of the pole. *Your sister is tied to the top of this pole. You can climb it and take her back. She has been sleeping, waiting for you.* The boy went to the pole, stood on his hind legs, grasped the wood with his hands, and began pulling himself up. The wolf paws scratched uselessly against the pole. The boy began pulling himself up by strength of his hands alone, the claws on his hind feet scrambling below him. His arms ached. His fingers burned with the effort of pulling up his body. The pole slowly pivoted as he climbed, turning in the direction the earth turned. Looking up through the smoke hole he saw day and night revolving above him. He saw the stars blink on and off. He saw the sun modest behind its veil of light. He climbed and climbed until he thought his arms would lose their strength and he would fall. Looking down, the earth was a blue curve below him. A steady wind blew, but the pole did not sway; the pole slowly turned, and the boy turned with it as he climbed.

The pole ended when there was no more pole to climb. The boy found a bundle of leaves tied to the pole by dark twine. He bit through the twine, grasped the bundle in his jaws, and began to descend. He heard breathing inside the bundle.

When he reached the ground again the man said, *You've found her, but you cannot unwrap her from the leaves until you leave the forest. She has slept within those leaves all these years, dreaming a life on top of the pole. In that dream she grew up with her mother, who collected seeds from flowers, and sealed them in packets to sell to the farmers' wives. Her mother who was a weaver and taught her daughter to spin. She went to sleep hearing stories about her brother stolen by a man with no face, and her father who fell asleep and never woke up. To unwrap her now would wake her from her dream before the dream is over, before she has entered the woods and found her baby brother, her twin, and she would die. I give her back to you, but you must give me something in return.* The man walked over to the boy. *Open your mouth.* The boy rested the bundle of leaves on the ground and opened his mouth. The man took a chisel out of one of his coat's pockets, took a small hammer from the other, and placing the chisel end against a sharp tooth, knocked the tooth out. The boy yelped and scurried backward. The man held up the tooth before the dark veil covering his face. It looked like a little star in his hand. *A new needle,* he said, and turning away from the boy, walked over to the pile of leaves, and sitting down beside it, took two, and began silently sewing them together.

The boy gently bit the bundle so he could hold it as he ran, and left the circular hut. His baby sister swung back and forth as he loped through the woods. He listened to her breathing while she slept, stirring slightly in her dream. He knew he must find the edge of the forest, but he knew the forest had no edge. He saw the woods through the wolf's eyes, knew what paths to wander. He heard through the wolf's ears and knew each sound's source. As the wolf, he was of the woods he wandered within.

One day, as dusk came on, he entered into the clearing that held the pond. He went down to the edge and lapped up some water, seeing in the crystalline depths the leafless tree emerge. When the moon rose and threw its circle on the water, he thought he saw a figure in the water, sleeping on a branch. He stared down into the water a long time, wondering if the moon was playing a trick on him. He listened to the baby breathe in the bundle of leaves. He had no time, he thought, for wonder. He heard all around him, suffusing the whole woods with music, the thorn woman's song, no single voice singing, but a voice that collected every voice in the woods and sang the countless parts into a single world. *When time begins again,* he thought, *the song will end.* The wolf he was belonged to the woods, not to time. To leave, the boy thought, he must take off the skin he wore, must see again with human eyes, hear with human ears. *The edge of the woods will be where silence begins, where light begins,* the boy thought. He sat back on his haunches, soothed by the sound of his sister's sleep, and while staring down in the water, nipped with his teeth at his navel, and began to undo the stitches in the wolf's skin. He began at the belly, tearing through the seam. From a distance, it looked as if a wolf was devouring itself, but no other eyes watched him at his work. Stitch by stitch the skin came undone. He heard his little sister moving within the leaves, her hands scratching against their underside. Her dream, too, was ending. He stared at the moon when it stood at the edge of the pond, a little door to another world, but not a world for him. He stared at the moon on the water and untied his throat.

A Point That Flows

1. THE SCULPTURE GARDEN

The people walked across the surface of the koi pond. The fish static beneath the water—keeping their place against the machine that produced the current—looked like orange kites filled with wind. The footbridge crossing the highway reflected on the water. I found the angle accidentally, walking in circles around the pond after teaching, conjuring the conversation again, replaying the small failures, the half-glimpsed ideas that promised secrets but led nowhere, the retreat to rhetoric—"What does it mean?" The day's lesson was on Platonic philosophy. Spiritual geometry. Forms and shadows. Looking down I saw up. Workers and tourists stepping across the water, the impossible traffic of the day stepping on the backs of the ornamental fish below them, neither aware of the other's presence, a slight wavering of both when a breeze rippled over the pond's surface. The eye a little pivot between worlds. The surface of the pond like the surface of a page: a thin boundary dividing above from below. To touch a woman would be to reach through her and scare the fish below. Both worlds were mine to see so long as I did not move. When the streetlights came on they dropped their constellations on the pond, charting the cosmic zones, sodium-yellow spots whose brightness obliterated the vision of the world their influence controlled. Time to go home.

When I picked up my bag, filled with papers to grade, and turned my head from the pond to the path leading out of the sculpture garden, a pinpoint of white light caught my eye. Over the course of the weeks I'd been coming to the pond, I'd often noticed such aberrations in my vision. I explained the phenomenon as a kind of afterimage of the streetlights on the water's surface, and an extra susceptibility of my mind after an hour or more of my odd meditations. The light looked as if it hovered ten feet from me, levitating in the air at the exact height of my eye. Usually, the point was dull yellow, or a glowing purple. Tonight, though, the point of light was phosphorescent bright, almost painful to look at directly. The statues scattered through the garden lurked vaguely in the periphery: a reclining woman in silhouette; an immense cube balanced on a corner, though in the strange light its girth looked flimsy, a tracing paper shadow that a breath could blow away; and a lion, in the classical style, modeled after Delacroix's painting, lapping water from the gravel. I waited for my eye to adjust to the evening, but the light only grew in intensity, finally becoming almost painful, so bright a sympathetic ringing began in my ear, so bright I began to feel nauseous, weak kneed, and dropping my bag to the ground, I bent over, my hands on my knees, and when I stood up again, my eye could bear the light without blinking.

The light did not move when I moved; it was not evanescent. What I thought a trick of my eye was not a trick of my eye. The point seemed fixed, luminous. I orbited around it, nearing it with each circle, examining it from every angle. Within the piercing brightness I began to see a slow cycling of every color that, finally settling into a blue cast, or a violet one, would gain a sudden speed and return to white, and then slow again, settling into yellow, stilling into red. I neared it as I gazed, until I came close enough to hold it in my hand. Reaching toward it, my hand didn't glow with its light, nor did its brightness cast a shadow on the ground. My presence didn't affect it. Quite the opposite. As I neared it, the light seemed to affect me. My eyes dazzled but not blinded by this brilliance. I felt no heat emanating from it, but felt some other radiance, as one feels the slightest waves of water push against one's ankles when standing still in the shallows. In my mouth, the slightest taste of saline. As I cupped my hand underneath it as if to enclose it, I heard a low, almost inaudible drone, absolutely constant, without any variation in pitch, against which, it seemed to me, silence itself could be heard. As I bent my fingers around it, the point of light extended, drew itself out, as if to prove the old geometry: a line is a point that flows.

The line didn't glow with the same intensity as the point hovering in the air. It looked like the thinnest of glass tubes, seen not by virtue of its own luminescence so much as the strange ability to turn the darkness around it slightly convex, as if indenting the space in which the phenomena occurred. The line extended to a tree whose secondary branch extended horizontally over the ground and whose leaves hung down, as from a curtain, toward the ground beneath them. I followed the line. At every step memory cast in my mind images to stop my forward progress—or so it felt to me. I saw my deceased grandparents. I saw my mother sitting in a chair. I saw my wife and child at our dinner table. And when I reached the down-hanging leaves, I pushed them aside with my hand as one pushes aside a beaded curtain, and stepped into the darkness where the line led.

2. The Bedroom

I stepped through the leaves not to find the hedgerow blocking the sculpture garden from the north-driving traffic in the adjacent street, but found myself in a bedroom. Moments of true disorientation are marked by the sense of their absolute normalcy. The room was lit by a single oil lamp, bathing the room in a warm glow that deepened the red tints of the woodwork around the windows. The faint line I followed into the room was still visible—if "visible" did justice to its actual appearance—bisecting the room, and pointing through the middle of a painting hanging on the wall furthest from me. The painting depicted a field of upturned sillion's shine, purple loam, and a child casting seed in the furrow. Opposite, facing a window reflecting the lamp sitting before it, was a desk that I looked at and considered my own. Opposite the desk, a bed—and in the bed, a woman.

Language fails beauty in expressing it. Is it enough to say: she slept. Enough that beneath her eyelids her eyes rolled, caught in a dream that quickened her fingers against her palms, that broke open the closed line of her lips, and then, in a sudden calm I could not guess at, her mouth closed, her eye stilled, and only the slight, quick pulsing at her neck marked the danger just passed. The bedsheets were pushed in a heap to the bottom of the bed. Only then did I notice that the window was open, that I could hear the wind move through the pines a distance away, could even hear the pinecones knock gently against each other like dull, wooden bells. Her breast was a shadow beneath the thin gown. The fabric rested against her skin as a fog rests against the ground, half-revealing the form it covers and which gives it shape. The longer I looked at her the less easy I grew. I thought: something in all beauty horrifies. As I watched this woman I became less and less convinced that she breathed. I heard no inhalation. I heard no sigh. Her chest neither rose nor fell. The vivid dream was gone. Every other appearance promised the most vital life—the tint of her cheek, the small animal motions of sleep, the finger that twitches and then curls out of itself. But I feared she was a corpse, or some sort of pupal life, deathlike before returning to life, a body without breath, and to break the spell of my growing hysteria, I turned away toward the desk and sat down.

I knew without searching which drawer contained some blank pages. I knew where to find the pen and ink. The light from the lamp glowed against the impressed edges of some script etched into the wood, as if the woman, or whoever sat here to write, had once been in such haste to record her thoughts that she took a single sheet of paper and pushed the letters through the page she wrote on. I ran my fingers across the surface and pulled out a sheaf of pages bound by twine looped through a hole in the pages' middle, so that the binding pierced the notebook's center. I caught my reflection in the window. I appeared in silhouette: no eyes, no mouth, no features. I looked as if I were leaving the room as I sat in it, and instead of my face gazing back into my own eyes, I was watching the back of my head as I departed. Time leaped ahead of itself. The present moment never reaching the present moment. I couldn't escape the growing sense that my life was occurring elsewhere, ahead of me, lived by a self who I was but who I couldn't be. I felt as if I were my own memory of myself. I was not living a life already lived, so much as a life that stepped forward into the past: memory as an open, indefinite realm, the impossible fact never eased by knowing the future it caused, as if an impenetrable screen drew across my vision, across my mind, separating wholly my life lived from my living life. Cause without consequence. The beauty behind me stirred, alive in her dream. I opened a drawer to take out a pen and ink and saw a brass letter opener, the cutting edge shaped like a crow's feather, the handle like a talon. It had a surprising heft, and the edge that tore open envelopes, cutting my finger as I ran it across, was honed needlessly sharp. I put it down and picked up the pen. I decided I should write down the events of the past hour, not trusting memory to remember, not trusting myself to recall the intricate knot of the day. I dipped the nib in ink and began: *The people walked across the surface of the koi pond.* As soon as I placed the period on the first sentence that came to mind, almost a kind of vision of a sentence, not even written by me who wrote it, I heard a voice from behind me.

"You're back? You just left and now you're back?" The woman had awoken.

"I'm not back. I just arrived. You were sleeping. You didn't hear me come in. My name is—"

"I know your name. Why would you tell me your name?"

"I think there's some kind of mistake. I followed a line—"

"Do you mean a road?" Her voice was unlike any voice I'd ever heard. It sounded as if a chorus spoke from her throat, the high pitch of a child's voice above the low, rasping tone of an old woman, and the middle ground filled out the harmony with a young woman's voice.

"Not a road. A kind of line—it's hard to explain."

"It's not hard to explain at all. That's just as you described it when you left. I can faintly see it myself. If I stare at it directly, it disappears.

But if I let my vision relax and stare at the wall without any desire to see the wall, I can see the line in the corner of my eye. You said you could see it directly, and so you should follow it. You thought it was a sign. And so you left."

"Where was I going?"

"You said you were going to the fields, going to war, going to the river beneath the pond . . . you spoke about ice in relation to time, about bees, about trees, about pollen's relation to the bodies that bear it, about the physiognomy of wind, about the clouds as bodies . . . you spoke of other things, unmentionable things, secrets between us, intimacies . . . you spoke of other women as other worlds . . . you were pale as you spoke . . . you spoke as if in a fever . . . you stared at me . . . I could see the vibration in your eyes . . . words. . . ." She spoke with her head on her pillow, her eyes closed, as if still within the dream she'd awoken from. "You'd been acting strangely for days. You turned the mirror against the wall. You said you were leaving. But now you're back."

"I'm not back. You've confused me with someone else."

She was silent for a moment. She closed her eyes. I expected her to sigh, but she sat deathly still, her hands on either side of her, dead weight against the mattress. The delicacy of her fingers mesmerized, the marble hue, the faint lines around her knuckles like crackle in porcelain, the lacustrine depth of her nails. Her hands looked as if they weighed more than themselves, as if they were anchors to keep her bound to the bed. Then, in her uncanny voice, she said, in a tone of absolute defeat, "You always tell me I've confused you with someone else. You always tell me that. You tell me I've made a mistake. You say it every time you return. If you'd just come to me, kiss me, lie down with me, you'd remember. You'd stop playing your games with me. You'd be at home with me, and life could be again what you'd promised when you brought me here, when you convinced me to leave my old home, in which I never had to suffer being alone."

"I don't know what to say."

"Say what you usually say. Blame me for your misfortune. Grow angry. Begin your rant. You know the one. 'The larval self, the pupal self, the exuviae of self, the slough of self, the imago of self, the winged self.' Your theories you write for hours at your desk, mumbling to yourself, sleepless, always on the 'verge of discovery,' say what you always say, or what you said before you left, when you grabbed the pages and lit them on fire and ran out the door with them burning in your hand, saying, 'The pages are part of the disease.' Say what you always say, and then run out the door." As she said this she lifted one hand very slowly, as if doing so required all the effort her body could muster, and pointed at a door in the wall. I hadn't noticed the door. It was as if her pointing at it created it, as if, in begging me to stay, she also implored me to leave, and provided the means for me to do so. I could faintly see the line I followed here. It pierced through the painting of the field that now seemed like the scenery through the window on the door.

The door had no knob. I just pushed against the wood and the door swung noiselessly open into the night. The new atmosphere rushed in, and crossing the threshold, I looked back and saw that the woman had lain back down and pulled the sheets up against the night air that settled down upon her, outlining her body with an unnatural accuracy, as if the sheets too possessed an unexplainable weight, and were woven, impossibly enough, from stone.

3. THE FIELD

How imperceptibly the eyes adjust to dimness is only revealed by the sudden step into unexpected brightness. In walking through a door

I stepped from midnight into noon, as if the doorframe's lintel were all that separated day from night. I found myself on the crest of a hill, a valley stretching out beneath me. I could still see the line that led me here: a thin concavity of blue against the blue sky. The line maintained its elevation, and to follow the road that led down the hill would take me away from it. I had little choice but to leave the line behind.

The road curved down the hill into the valley, splitting an orchard in two. The orchard, from my elevation, looked like white blossoms dropped by a child in rows, as if, in substitution for toy soldiers, a boy had stolen his mother's bouquet and used the flowers to fill the ranks. The hill itself was covered in long grasses, creased in the middle. I picked one—unconsciously folding and unfolding the leaf—as I walked along. The heat of the day increased as I descended. No wind blew. The clouds were anchored in the sky. The dust settled behind my step. I stepped through the stillness of the world; I was the only moving thing. The dusty road silenced my motions. I heard no buzzing as of bees. I saw no butterflies, no moths. I had to speak my name to myself to break the silence.

The lower the path led me the closer the orchard came. As the time passed, as the miles passed, as I walked closer and closer to the orchard, the single flowers seen from such a height expanded as I neared, radiating from their centers, clusters of blossoms separating from the singular mass, the unseen sweep of the curving branches visible in the sweep of the flowers, proximity revealing details the next steps proved were but vague abstractions in which more delicate features hid; and the white blossoms, each composed of intricately entwined flowers whose shape mimicked exactly the shape of the larger whole, as if the atomic structure of the plant, could it be seen, would reveal the same tri-petal form in microscopic size, the labyrinth of the plant not a result of difference, but the never ceasing repetition of the same form. I remembered, when I finally entered the grove, and walking to a tree, inhaled the scent of the flower, a film from my school-age days, in which a single point inwardly glowing, but glowing as if with darkness rather than light, expanded over the course of an hour into the universe that made possible my own viewing of the birth of the universe. The flower's scent was most discernable for its lack of scent. I felt as if breathing in the blossom made me more aware of the lack of scent in the air around me, and the fragrance was no fragrance, a lack perfuming lack.

In that vacuum of sound, of scent, a noise suddenly startled me. I heard a faint shuffling of feet. Listening closer, another sound, as of the shaking of leaves. I stood still, looking around me, and as I did, the sounds grew louder, until I heard, faintly but unmistakably, a voice humming three notes in long, repetitive drone; and behind the tune, if it can be called a tune, I saw a boy. He looked hypnotically engaged in his work: grasping the stem of a blossom, holding a page beneath it, shaking the flower gently, looking at the page and carefully bending the page along a central fold, pouring what fell from the blossom into a bag lashed to his side. I worried I would startle him. But when he came to the tree I was standing below, he simply looked at me, no change of expression on his face, and asked me: "Why are you here?"

"I walked down the hill."

"Which hill?"

I pointed back along the direction from which I had come. He looked off toward the horizon. "You came from the west?" he asked.

"I suppose so."

"We're all waiting for the men to return. But they walked east." He pointed further along the road I had been walking on. "But no one ever walks back from the east. Not yet." He stepped to the branch nearest him, grasped the flower, put the page underneath it, and shook. A fine dust fell onto the white page, tinted black, so that it looked as if the page held its own ash.

"What are you doing?"

"I'm collecting the pollen from the trees in the orchard. This orchard is my job. Other children are in other orchards, and many of them are in the fields, shaking the grains."

"Why?"

"You know. The bees."

"The bees?"

"Yes. The bees are gone. The bees are gone and now we have to pollinate all our food. The men showed us what to do before they left, and then they left."

"Why did they leave?"

The boy looked at me quizzically, seeing me, it felt, for the first time, as if by my question, I startled him out of the stupor of his work. "You aren't from here?"

"No. I'm from—"

"The bees are gone," he said, this time with emphasis. "Back behind the orchard are the hives we keep, built by our ancestors, interconnected, in which a single queen harmonized the activity of every worker. The men cared for the bees."

"What happened? Why are there no bees now?"

"The queen is gone."

"She died?"

"I don't know. The voice arrived and the next day the queen was gone. Then all the workers flew in circles. Some still are flying in circles. They die as they fly. We'd find them on the ground. Now hardly any are left. Sometimes you see one in the air, a little black dot in the sky, flying in a circle. The voice came and the queen disappeared. The men opened the central hive where she lived—a thing forbidden for us to do. They opened the hive and found the queen's chamber empty, each wall coated with a dust, a stony dust."

"What voice?"

"You don't hear it?"

"Your voice is the first voice I've heard since I've been here."

"The voice in the air? Declaring the war? They erected an antenna far away, and it transmits the voice—that's what the men say. 'There's a war,' it says. It says, 'Your freedom is threatened.' It says, 'Join us. Join us,' it says, and 'Be a hero.' Our men walked east. Some wanted to join the war. Many of the men wanted to be heroes. I want to be a hero but I'm too young. I'm too young to hear the voice, the men said. Some people said the queen obeyed the voice, and some people said the voice killed the queen. Some said the frequency of the transmission confused her, or hurt her, or drove her away. Some people say she disappeared, and that old stories, stories never told now, said this has happened before, and because we've forgotten the story, we don't know what to do. Some of the men went away to join the war, and some went away to find the antenna and destroy it. But they left a long time ago, and no one's returned."

He looked at me for a long time. I thought he was going to ask me a question, but he put his hand out, reaching toward my face, not to touch it, but as if he wanted to see my head from a certain angle, as a distant relative might, to find the family resemblance. But he drew his hand back, turned toward the tree beside us, and began his work again. And, not knowing what else to do, I returned to the path and continued my walk eastward. Silence returned. When I rose out of the orchard, I took another piece of grass and rolled it around my finger, like a ring. It took a long time to reach the top of the hill. Above me, I found the line, a blue concavity against the blue, maintaining its elevation, lost again in the sky as I gazed after it, and looking down in the next valley, saw the gray clouds obscuring the land into which I now must enter.

4. THE TOWN

The air smelled different in the new valley. The closer I came to the cloud-enveloped town, the more dingy the gray fog grew. Yellowish wisps took shape and rolled through the darker cloud dispersing again into the miasma. Something fetid in the air, a bog somewhere at the periphery, bugs clicking like empty rifles firing, the hammer hitting the chargeless plate; such was their mating song. A bird emerged from the dust as my foot neared it, scared out of its nest, two eggs mimicking stones in a shallow depression, the bird edging backward from me, slowly dragging one wing through the dirt as it were broken, luring me away from the nest. To be seen as a predator made me feel like one. I thought about stepping on the eggs, watching the yolk spill out; my own desire horrified me. I saw myself as the threat. When I had passed it I turned around and watched it move back to its brood, settle into the dust, and disappear.

I don't know how long I walked before I reached the outskirts of the town. The grain in the outlying fields had been trampled, in areas scorched, so that the charcoal looked like the shadows, clouds cast on the ground, but darker. Somewhere cinders smoldered. A cow stood at the edge of the singe, grazing. Next to it another cow lay dead, eviscerated. Crows fought in the entrails, scavenging augers. I kept walking down the road that cut the fields in two. The dust gave way to crude macadam, the bitumen acrid in the air. The fog clung smoke-like to the ground. No demarcation separated the rural from the town. Gradually I found myself walking on cobblestones, houses and storefronts on either side of me. Many of the buildings were burned or still burning. Even in the dull light the broken glass gleamed. A cart had been turned over in the middle of the town square. It had been carrying ice in large, straw-insulated crates. Now blocks of ice, larger than a tall man, broken through the wood, stood on the street among the windblown straw. The ice possessed an oddly blue hue. It looked as if blocks of the firmament had fallen randomly to the ground, and people gathered around to watch the sky melt.

I stepped among them; for a long while no one looked at me, thinking me another of the town. But then a young girl looked up, focused on my face, lifted her arm, and pointing at me, began to cry. The others looked up. The women grabbed their children and stepped back from the ice, stepped back from me. One man came forward, raising his hand in preparation, I thought, to strike me, but two other men held him back; he struggled against their arms, pushing against their hands, but they wouldn't relent, and they pulled him away, down the street, into a storefront with a broken window. A young woman, younger than me, stared at me, tears running in straight lines down her pale face, her eyes wide, not blinking, the cornea tinted slightly blue, like the ice in the street. She pulled a locket from inside her blouse, and clutching it in her hand, stepped solemnly toward me, unclasped the locket, and held in front of my face the picture of a young man; the locket shook slightly: the pulsing in her hand, the beating of her heart, her breathing. She opened her mouth; I thought she was going to speak to me, explain to me. . . . But, link by link, she let the locket slowly lower from her grasp, until she held it by a last gold circlet; the locket moved in a slow circle; and then, with a motion that seemed impossibly slow, she opened her fingers and the locket dropped. Then the young woman turned on her heels and ran down the street.

I picked up the locket and yelled after her, "Please, wait!" I followed her, the necklace in my hand. I didn't run; I couldn't bring myself to run. I could feel the eyes of the townspeople on me. My heart, though, beat frantic in my throat. I could feel in myself a menace I could not explain. I couldn't see where she had run to, into which building or alley she had turned. I heard doors slam as I walked down the street. I heard men yell for their families to stay inside. I saw a body facedown on the sidewalk. A horse galloped blindly from a side street, rearing up on its hind legs and kicking out with the front, striking at an enemy that did not exist and then bounding away in the direction it had sprung from, an eye missing from its socket. I slowed my pace. I could feel something in the air, as an animal feels a storm before a cloud forms. The air felt thicker, full with some electric potential. I realized for many minutes I'd been hearing a low buzzing in my ear. Far down the street I saw a structure. With the locket in my hand, I walked toward it. At first I thought it was a shed, but as I neared it, its bulk from a distance turned into scaffolding whose substance was the shadow that the platform threw below it. One block away, I saw it was a gallows. Half a block away I saw a man standing on the gallows. His back was to me, a thin line vertical above his head. Then the pencil-thin line expanded into a rope, and the rope circled his neck. I walked up the steps to the platform and stood behind him. I thought I would remove the noose and leave the town; walk away in the direction the man was staring. But, hearing my steps behind him, he spoke: "Is it you?"

"I don't know," I answered. I stepped in front of him, to see his face.

"It is you. You've returned. Just as you said you would."

"You've made a mistake," I said. My voice sounded cold to me, without emotion, numb.

"So you told me when you put this noose around my neck."

"I never put a noose around your neck."

"So you said as you tightened it. You said my own deeds have done this to me, not you. You said you were acting for justice, which could not act for itself."

"What have you done?"

The man was silent, staring at me. I stared back. Slowly, vaguely, I realized I'd seen him before, I recognized him. I opened my hand, and then I opened the locket. His face was in my hand, encircled in gold; and looking up, his face before me, his neck encircled with rope. "You asked me that before, and when I had no answer, you told me you'd return, and when you did, I must confess, and if I confessed, you could dismiss the sentence you declared against me."

I cannot say how I felt hearing the man speak; there are no words for a horror that ceases to be horror in becoming real. I said to him, again, "What have you done?"

"I don't know what I've done. I worked in the fields. I fell in love. I read books. I lusted. I enjoyed my food and drink. I tried to be kind. I fought against the army. I killed a nameless man who was my enemy. I prayed at night and then gave up praying. I sought solace in the body of my wife. I don't know what I've done. I've lived my life like other men live theirs. I don't want to beg for my life from you, but I will: Spare me. Let me stay."

I listened, and when he finished speaking, I closed the locket, and drawing both hands simultaneously away from it, extended the chain to its full diameter. He closed his eyes, and slowly, almost imperceptibly, shook his head back and forth. His chin quivered slightly, and then, as if gathering a final strength, he calmed down, the line of his jaw eased; he tilted his head up and opened his eyes. His left eye was so dark I couldn't differentiate the pupil from the iris. But his right eye glowed with the brilliant light I saw in the sculpture garden, the light that led me here. He stared at me, unaware, I think, of the brilliance in his eye, unaffected by it, looking at me as if I was fate or fury, as if I were judging him. His eye was its own justice. It seemed as if his eye had changed its nature, and all the light that in a lifetime poured into the little hole, collected in the brain, bridging the distance between stars and selves, reached some terminal capacity and, reversing in the mind, shone out from what it had entered. I looked at him and began to cry. I wanted to ask him his forgiveness. I reached my arms toward him, as if to embrace him, and put around his neck the locket stretched between my hands, and as soon as the locket rested against his chest, my arms on either side of his face, the trapdoor beneath his feet sprang open, and together, we fell down into the shadow below.

5. The Salt Flat

The shadow ended in brightness; I ended up alone. I looked up, fearing I'd see the man's feet dangling above me, suspended by the rope, but saw only the deep blue sky domed solid above me, light piercing through the vault, obliterating shadow. Not that any object existed to cast a shadow, save myself. I was standing on a vast salt flat, horizon in every direction. A thin surface of water stood on the surface of the salt. When I looked down at my feet the water was transparent and I could see the minute particles of the salt underneath the surface, but looking up, the water became a mirror to the sky above it, so that, gazing around me, I stood in the center of the sky, heaven above and heaven below, stretching indefinitely in every direction to the horizon, a limit unseeable, where the body of the sky and the sky's image cinched shut. I began walking; I didn't know what else to do. I took a step in the direction I was facing, and continued into vertigo not of height but of horizon, of lack of horizon, of no marker in the field of sight to judge distance gained, so that all distance felt like no distance at all, and every motion left me in the center, from which one could not escape, from which I could not escape. I walked, stepping on the sky below my feet, haunted by the feeling that another self was walking above me, his head balanced precisely on my head, his step matching my step, his thought matching my thought, except his feet stepped on some ground now denied me, dust or grass or gravel, and I stepped into the air through which I could not fall. I began to fear the next motion. Glancing ahead as the blue stretched out in equal depth above me and below me, so that up and down lost sense as oppositions, I felt the next moment could be the one in which I plummeted—a fall up or a fall down—not to my death, for what is death in such a world as this one, but fell without limit, without time, forever. So much did this paranoia affect me, agitate my nerves, that I found myself paralyzed, unable to, or unwilling to, take one more step. I stood still and stared at the missing horizon, my head aching from the glare, absolutely alone, not knowing if I looked down when I bent my head, or up, until at the furthest extreme I'd see my own feet, my legs, my hands and arms, and looking the opposite direction, see no body at all. And it was then, staring up into the blue surrounding me, that I saw the line. The line could hardly be discerned from the blue around it. Its character, or its nature, seemed to have changed. It no longer bore a trace of the radiance from which it flowed, nor did it seem a thin glass spicule visible by containing the element it pierced through, a shard of hollow ice in water, now it looked meager, looked miniscule, a pencil line perfectly straight, or a taut, black thread.

My only hope was that the line that had led me here would lead me away from here. I followed it. To fight the vertigo I watched my feet as I walked, keeping my eye on the salt beneath me, watching as the saline water thickly rippled with my motion, and so rippled, briefly, to an extent, the sky. But I could not see the thread in the reflected sky below me, and found that I veered unintentionally away from my trajectory, tending naturally into a curve, and if I didn't look up at regular intervals, I would lose myself. I walked, rhythmically inclining my head upwards, then inclining my head down, witnessing the sky, witnessing my body, ceaselessly, the action a kind of mantra, almost a kind of prayer. Vision interrupting vision. Thought unspooled into memory and memory into mindlessness, into myth, into timelessness, a self below the self, a fungal contemplation among the bones. My journey stretched out in my mind, a mural painted on a winding sheet. Who was this me others met? Who was this me sentencing others to death? Sending the beekeepers to the war? Whose voice was this voice? Whose wife this woman? I walked and the questions repeated, lost meaning, the words losing sense, the syntax undone, the grammar buried in the folds of deeper meaning, until the self became a drone singing beneath the thought of itself, and it was then, at that moment in which thought ceased to be recognizable as thought, that I realized I had come to destroy myself. One would think, or so I would have thought, that suicide solved the problem. A man drowns in surfaces and shallows and does not need depths to drown. But the self with which I had to grapple was the self outside of me, this other self, it seems, I am.

I walked. I do not know for how long I walked. Night never came, but days passed. There was time here, but what was time here? I walked and walked. And then, in the midst of my endless head tilting, my eye caught what looked like a speck of dust, just a speck of dust, no larger, that marked for the first time the horizon. The thin thread above me led toward it, and so, ceasing to bend my head up and down, I focused on the dot in the distance and walked toward it. Slowly, slowly, it grew larger—it was not evanescent. It was fixed, or if not fixed, nearing me as I neared it. It was hard to tell who moved, what moved. The mote elongated, a sapling, but a sapling in motion, then thicker, as if the sapling were springing into mature form, and then the tree in motion, branches moving, not as pushed by the wind, but by its own volition, until the tree became a man walking toward me as I walked toward him. I didn't increase my pace, nor did he. The glare kept him in silhouette, and now, as near him as I was, I felt as if I were walking to meet a shadow. When he was but a fathom from me, he reached out a hand as I reached out mine. I felt like my eyes couldn't adjust to the light, couldn't clarify his features even at such proximity. He must suffer the same problem, as neither of us slowed, nor did we slow when the eyes came into focus, and the face around them, nor at our mutual shock as we saw who the other was, nor did I stop until my held-out hand, in reaching for his, rested against the surface of the mirror.

I didn't cry or speak or scream. I simply held my hand against the image of my hand, and stared into my own eyes. I worried he wasn't only a reflection, but that, on the mirror's other side, he was facing me in the same bewildered regard I was beholding him. I saw behind both of me the blue distance I had walked across. I could not tell what was reflection and what real, what an image and what an object. The thin, dark thread or line was above me, piercing into the mirror's surface but not reflected in the mirror itself, and it was then, thoughtlessly, without will, I turned my hand against the reflection of my hand, and a door in the mirror opened, and I walked in.

6. ON A STAIR

Such dark after such bright blinded me. My ear saw before my eye: low, cyclical thrum. As I heard my eye adjusted. The sound emanated from a dark orb spinning above my head. The orb darkly glowed with the color of a lightning strike at night when the lightning remains only in the eye. It didn't rotate in any single direction, but rotated in every direction at once, spooling onto itself countless threads that, glowing themselves, joined the phosphorescent luster without adding to the orb's brightness or bulk. The line I followed here was one such thread, now lost to me among the multitude. The eerie glow from the orb cast a faint light, and I saw, sitting, it seemed, on a stair, a girl reading a book. I walked over to her. She sat partway up a stair which ascended out of sight, a stair whose descent I couldn't gauge, as the ground I stood on seemed to have little relation to the stairs themselves, as if the floor, like the orb above it, hovered on a plane of its own hidden nature. The girl looked up when I neared.

"Hello," she said.

"Where am I?" I asked her.

"That's not really a question I can answer."

I didn't know what else to say. The world had left behind the fact of itself.

"What is your name?" I asked.

"No one calls me by a name. I sit on these stairs," and saying so, she swept her arm in a circle, implying there were more stairs inclining away from this point in every direction, "and read."

"What are you reading?"

"A book that told me you would be coming soon."

"Have you seen me before? Do you know me?"

"It's a strange book," she said, ignoring my question. "The face of every open page is blank, but the pages underneath those I look at are filled with words. Turn a page over, and the words are gone. But I've learned to read by a certain light that sees through a page to read a page. And beneath this page," she held up the book which, as she described, was open to blank pages, "it said you'd arrive."

"I am here to—"

"I know why you're here. No one comes here for a reason other than yours."

"Then tell me where to find—"

"I can't do that. I'm just a girl who sits on the stairs and reads. I know little more than that you'd come, that we'd talk."

As I looked at her the stairs gained definition.

"Am I supposed to walk up these stairs, these stairs you're sitting on?"

"I don't know what you're supposed to do."

I stepped onto the staircase and climbed to where she sat. I looked at the book she was reading and saw beneath the right-hand page a few disconnected though discernable words:

> *The people*   *the surface of*
>
> *water*

>
>   *reflected on*   *water*

When she saw I was reading the page beneath the page, she closed the book.

I looked up the stairs I was ascending, but had yet to take another step. It was a comfort being near the girl. I wanted to sit next to her, to learn to read the book she was reading.

"You cannot read this book," she said. "It isn't allowed." She didn't say this with reprobation or regret. She spoke as one recites a law.

I craned my neck upwards, straining to see where the stairs led. The darkness gradually changed. What I saw seemed to me a trick of the eye, as happens when one stares too long in the darkness, or as a child amuses himself by pressing on his closed eyes to see the sudden, inexplicable lights playing against the screen of his own lids, lost in the little cosmos. Far above me, a dimness of light in the dimness of dark, I saw orange circles floating in slow circles, a perimeter of liquid light around them all, and dimmer even than those, a light-colored smudge, oval in shape, floating as a leaf suspended in the air that, to me who was staring up at it, seemed to be staring back down.

Apology for the Astrolabe

M. was born with a birthmark that covered the upper-half of his back. As a child, the mole was thick—a dark pillow on his skin. As he grew older the birthmark became covered with hair. The hair was black and gray—as if, even in adolescence, he was an aging man—and soft. Every year the hair grew thicker, became more interbraided, more intertwined, until it appeared as if M. had a prayer rug stitched to his back. This is exactly how M. thought about his curious malady: I am a man with a prayer rug on my back. M. liked to watch TV sitting on his couch. He kept on the couch's arm a back scratcher, a thin piece of wood at the end of which a wooden hand was stapled. M. watched the TV and scratched his back which, especially in the summer, could grow quite itchy. The TV this summer was always the same broadcast carried on every channel that M. could get in clearly: the trials in Nuremberg. It was not the 1940s. The grandchildren, and in some cases the great-grandchildren, were being prosecuted for the crimes of their Nazi ancestors. The police didn't apprehend these young men and women. They turned themselves in. They demanded the trial. They held protests, held strikes, threatened violence until their demands were met. Now they sat in the witness stand while the jury listened, and as the prosecutors, in ever increasing detail, explained to them the atrocity of their own lineage. The TV cameraman would spend a long time in close-up on the faces of the prosecuted. Eyes open or closed, crying quietly or not crying, looking down while nodding head in recognition of some fact previously lost or suppressed. For many nights now the news clip highlight was of a young man, almost offensively handsome, turning to the jury and saying to them: I am guilty.

Those pronounced guilty sentenced themselves. Many gave away their fortunes, an attempt at reparation. They found comfort, they said in posttrial interviews, in returning something to the families from which almost everything had been stolen. But others, such as the handsome young man in today's trial, scoffed at such notions as an easy route to absolution. Such men and women sentenced themselves to death. The viewing audience could call in and vote on their agreement with the judgment. A live tally was kept in a yellow ribbon at the bottom of the screen. Tens of thousands of people called in. Most would overturn the sentence the defendant decreed against himself—a fact M. attributed to the show's deeper work: a forum to end a guilty inheritance. The defendant was contractually obligated to adhere to the public's appeal. At the end of the show, the con-demned would walk past the gallows—often pale, often visibly shak-ing—constructed in the courtroom itself, from whose terror he had just been remanded.

M. had the number on speed dial on his phone, but he never could bring himself to call in—not because of any indignation, but because he could never make up his mind how to vote. He scratched his back and thought through the arguments, a kind of thinking inevitably subject to the habitual distraction of M.'s mind. Thinking about guilt and innocence he found himself considering the electronic waves speeding through the air by which the show arrived in his TV. The handsome young man who sentenced himself to death was in the air, fully articulate if one had the right kind of antenna. M. supposed the air was filled with all sorts of wavelengths that in any given moment penetrated his body—but that, lacking the right apparatus, were only silent to him. As he scratched his back watching the credits roll across the screen he thought about the voices articulate but unheard in the air. The atmosphere was haunted; the ears and eyes haunted, but the mind deaf and blind to the frequency in which the ghosts spoke. The TV cast its pale light into the room, a kind of sun setting one could turn off with a button.

When the phone rang M. knew it would be his mother. She wanted to know the night's verdict. She couldn't watch the show since she began her new job. She was in her seventies and shouldn't be working, but the medical expenses had destroyed her retirement savings. Now she worked evenings—the dinner hours—for a tele-marketing firm selling a duct-vacuuming service which promised to decrease allergic reactions in every family by 40 percent. Money-back guarantee. Did you know how much dust collected in the ducts of our houses? Blowing through the vents with the heated air, settling on everything, in everything. Most of the dust was human skin, pet dander, grass pollen, and mold. A child growing up in such a house harms herself with every breath. It was a pretty good argument, M. thought. That dust didn't only come from the family living in their house, but from every family who had ever lived in that house. That invisible proof of lives completely unknown, save for the irritation in the throat and eyes caused by their skin which still clung to the ductwork of the walls long after their lives had ended. To sneeze in the springtime is a form of possession, M. thought, as he told his mother the night's verdict: guilty, a death sentence commuted by the world at large.

"Guilty!" his mother croaked, "I knew it. They're all guilty, each one of them." Since the surgery, M.'s mother had lost all intonation in her voice. He never knew when she was joking and when not.

"How's the night, Mom?"

"Sold three full-cleans, and one 'free inspection.' No one else sold more than one." M. hoped his mother's coworkers appreciated her delight at her own success.

Oddly, the tracheotomy seemed to have helped his mother's tele-marketing career. When she called in the midst of some family's cas-serole, TV turned on to the trials or the game shows or the sports highlights, the poor man or woman or child who answered must have thought Death herself was calling to offer a chance to have the house's ductwork returned to an original quality of hygiene. The strange es-sence of the voice, spoken in a low, rumbling, toneless drone—so that the words were hard to parse out from one another—was amplified by the pause between holding the speaker to her throat and then shifting the receiver up to her ear to listen to the answer. The silences were unnerving—even for M. But, contrary to M.'s own predictions, his mother sold more duct cleanings than any other employee, had been employee of the month two times in a row, lorded the privileged parking spot over her coworkers, and walked into the office every morning to see a gilt-framed photo of herself on the wall, the little white tube in the center of her throat.

"How's life?" she asked. [Pause.]

"Life's good, Mom." [Pause.]

"Not life. I mean how's business? You making any money? Why not give up on your schemes and come work with me?" M.'s mother had been pressuring him to give up his 1-800 number since he started.

"I should go, Mom. Thanks for the call. People start calling after the show. It's my busy time of the day." And in the midst of his mother's croaking rebuttal M. hung up the phone.

. . .

All the get-rich-quick schemes had failed: the hair-growth stimulant from the Colombian scientist (country, not university), the investment in vegetarian pepperoni, the bobble-head religious figures (Buddha, Moses, Christ, a Wiccan wood spirit, and most impressively, M. thought, a Burning Bush on which the flame bounced up and down) for the dashboard of cars, and all the others. M. wasn't on the verge of homelessness nor starvation. The inheritance he received from his father's death had long-ago paid for the little bungalow M. lived in, and the annuity provided money for other necessities—as long as those necessities stayed necessities. It was a frugal, semiascetic life. But M. saw himself in a different light than his situation cast him in. He always felt, and felt even now—as he walked from the couch to the kitchen scratching his back—that he was destined for greatness. M. didn't like that term—"greatness" implying power or importance. M. felt he had a contribution to make whose effect extended past the meager boundaries of his own life. M. felt that he had a chance to belong. How'd he recognize that moment when his life slipped past the confines of only being himself and invisibly interpenetrated with the lives around him, he didn't know. When younger he thought it would feel like ecstasy; as a teenager, orgasm. Now—inexplicably—the same hope harbored a different manifestation. He imagined enlightenment as an irritation of the skin. He imagined an allergic reaction: the skin palpably reacting to the falsity of its own limits. He thought this thought while scratching the prayer rug on his back.

M. thought the onset of the trials, and the global media frenzy around them, offered a new chance to succeed. He bought a second phone line, a 1-800 number. The voice of the salesman had been smarmy, assuming the number would eventually connect to some sort of phone-sex operation. M. had pondered that thought a number of years ago, fearing that the majority of people's problems were rooted in sexual frustration—but imagining the conversations he'd have, and his own participation in them, dissuaded himself from the venture. This 1-800 number—1-800-367-4483, or 1-800-FOR-GIVE—allowed people to call and confess whatever guilt rattled through their consciences, and M.'s only role was to listen and say, "I forgive you." He thought about saying "We forgive you," but decided the singular was more intimate. Three weeks ago he'd taken out an ad in the local paper, a small square with the number and nothing else printed on it, rather humble looking among the ads for hydroponic tomato kits and urine-cleansing drug kits and requests for people to submit (for pay) to medical experiments and, highlighted in green vines whose print failed to be confined by the leaves' outlines, free medical marijuana for chronic sufferers of stress or headache.

The first call came the first day—around twilight, just after the trial had ended for the day:

"Hello?"

"Hello."

"So, I just saw the ad and so—I just tell you, you know . . . tell you, um, what happened?"

"Yes."

"My twin brother, well, he's always been the perfect son, and, um, I haven't. I haven't been so . . . good, you know, in the way he's good. I know my parents—they admire him. I use drugs—I don't even try to hide it. I'm so thin, I scare myself a little." The voice sounded young, a little bedraggled. "I kind of like, you know, feeling like others think I'm a screw-up—I kind of like feeling them judge me. Does that make sense?"

M. didn't say anything. He wasn't prepared to be drawn into conversation. He didn't want to feel like an accomplice in someone's guilt, but rather someone anonymous, some voice that spoke alone out of the ether, simply saying, as if speaking for the world or some force in the world, "I forgive you."

"Are you listening?"

M. hesitated. "Yes."

"Okay, um. So, I'm the screw-up, and my identical twin is golden. I use drugs; he eats, like, power bars. We're both about to graduate. Do you know what's weird? As a kid our teachers never knew who was who. And now, you know, no one mistakes us. No one does. I don't know why that bothers me. I think, you know, in the end, um— he and me—we're not able to be told apart. And, uh, this thought got stuck in my head—that I should see someone like me when I look at him. Like it used to be. He's applying for college. He might get an athletic scholarship. They've offered him one. Long-distance running. And it's a good school. His whole future, you know, what he's worked for. I'm working as a short-order cook. Just enough to keep my stash stashed. And, you know, you know, I knew he had a drug test for school—they make the athletes pee in a cup. His scholarship and all that? He has to pass the drug test first. He told me about it. And that afternoon, after school, I hung out by the door of the locker room, and when he came out, I went in, I found the cup with his name on it, dumped it down the sink, and took a piss in it myself. And that freed something in me. I mean, something broke in me. And I went home, turned on our computer, went into his files, and rewrote his college application essays. I wrote how 'I was looking forward to all the pussy—and that pussy would likely be my major.' I wrote other things. I just, you know, improvised—put in whatever seemed to fit with what he was talking about. And then I caught my own face in the screen, saw myself, you know, and deleted what I wrote. I saw my own face and couldn't believe what I'd done. I fixed the essay, but peeing in the cup? Too late. It's done. It's in the lab right now coming up positive. What do you think of that?"

"I forgive you."

"What?"

"I forgive you."

The boy was silent for a long time. M. could hear him breathing, but the boy didn't speak. M. didn't know if the boy felt relieved, felt cleansed, or felt the call was worthless, the forgiveness fraudulent. While M. waited he scratched his back. And after a minute of silence, the boy said, "Do you want me to hang up?" M. didn't know how to reply. And then the boy hung up.

. . .

The calls had no pattern, save that most came after the show ended, around twilight, as the sun was setting. M. began to think of conscience as dusk-colored—a time that is also a place, neither light nor dark, neither day nor night, a realm of impossible confusion, in which the world, or the self, could teeter toward either extreme. M. thought one possible result of twilight was day emerging again instead of night—a peculiar day in which the moon still rose, in which the stars could still be seen, but in which the dark wasn't dark. Something, he thought, could adjust in the eye, and night would cease to be night. People called for reasons profound and reasons less so. Eating too many cookies. Feeding pets poison. Setting a wedding dress on fire. Suffocating a baby sister in the crib. Forgetting someone's name. M. thought at one time he should keep track of why people called, but decided such notetaking countered his work. He was erasing the record, not keeping it. He was not conducting a study, but the opposite. M. was learning how to forget so others could forget. His was a work against memory. He kept a pen and notebook by the phone, and he kept it pointedly blank.

But the work wearied him. Not the fact that someone could call, and often would call, at 3:00 a.m. reeling, drunk, confessing some misdeed minor or horrific—sleeping with a friend's girlfriend, hitting someone in the car on the way home from the bar. What wearied M. was the growing sense that people most often called immediately after their misdeed, when their conscience was inflated by the immanence of guilt, and forgiveness pricked the pressure, stopped it from taking hold, from becoming a burden. M. had imagined forgiveness as something not bound by time, not of the day, but a force that reached back through one life to reach the lives before, parents and grandparents, ancestors, cleansing all the hands, even the hands that were no longer hands, those forgotten hands which made these living hands possible, those hands in the blood. To ask forgiveness betrayed the limit of the body, of the present, and reached back through a current life to all the lives before it, lives still pulsing in the veins of the living, lives without identity, without voice, haunting the body from within it. To ask forgiveness was to speak with every voice. It should surprise the one asking to not recognize the sound of one's own voice saying "I." Guilty chorus in the blood. Haunted song seeking forgiveness for everyone. But M.'s philosophy decayed day by day. People called and their guilt was a shiny surface, a moment, an indiscretion that troubled the film of the self by clouding it—and M.'s "I forgive you" felt like the moral equivalent of wiping a mirror clean with a rag. "I looked up my boss's skirt." "I forgive you."

. . .

As M. opened a beer and sat down at the table for the night's calls, he thought: I've failed again. He sipped his beer in one hand and scratched his back with the other. The summer's heat had irritated the prayer rug, which not only itched incessantly—almost maddeningly, making sleep difficult, making it difficult at times to think—the mole also pulsed as it itched, as if a surplus of blood welled up beneath it. He thought he'd not renew the number's contract when it the current one was up—next week or soon after. The typical calls came in. M. went to get another beer and the phone rang.

"Hello?"

"Is this the forgiveness hotline?"

"Yes."

"Good." The voice on the line sounded different than most of the voices M. heard. It lacked panic, or shame—he couldn't quite pin the difference down.

M. waited but the man on the phone didn't speak. Minutes passed. Those who called often took time to gather their courage before confessing—but the quality of this silence was different. The silence was silent. It had no tension in it, no anticipatory awkwardness. M. felt as if he were sleeping.

"A long time ago a man feared for his people. He lived in a city where he was a religious minority, and he was a leader among them.

The citizens of the town would attack his people, would maim them, would kill them. Lies abounded. Usurers and murderers. Some said his people stole babies from the citizens and used the babies' blood to leaven their bread. Accused them of atrocity in order to commit atrocity against them."

The man paused. M.'s back itched painfully, but he had stopped scratching it.

"This man knew he had no power to stop the citizens of the town, and he knew his words that were a comfort to his people were only words. And so, when the time seemed propitious, he went into an alley, pushed dirt into a pile, and over the course of the night chanted the letters of the alphabet, in order, in reverse, and then in every permuted combination possible. One mistake would ruin everything. One mistake, one repetition or one omission, and the earth he walked on in his meditations would open up and swallow him. But he made no mistakes, for he was a man of great faith and great concentration. And when he had finished, when every letter joined in speech every other letter, the pile of dirt stood up and was a man. This man had no soul. On his forehead was printed the word *emet*, which means *truth*. This dust man obeyed what he was told to do. He was told to protect. The dust man wandered through the streets of the town, protecting the persecuted people, rescuing them from danger. He never slept. He never grew weary. The people felt safe again, felt happy. But as he wandered, as he helped those who needed help, he also grew stronger, and his strength became dangerous. The man knew the dust man would soon harm the people he now helped. And so, finding him one evening in an alley not far from the alley in which he was created, this man took his hand and wiped away the first letter printed on the dust man's head, leaving only *met*. And as soon as the letter disappeared the dust man became again only a pile of dust."

"Yes," M. said, as if asking a question.

"Yes."

M. waited for the man to go on speaking, but the man said nothing more.

M. said, "Did you call to ask forgiveness?"

"No."

"Then why did you call?"

"I called to forgive you."

. . .

The next days passed in unease—not simply in the mind, but in the body. M.'s mole felt as if it were burning, as if the mat of hair thick on it were smoldering. The consistency of the pain made his thoughts inconstant. He felt distracted. His heart felt kaleidoscopic. M. struggled to hide the desperate sarcasm in his voice when, to those who kept calling, he said, "I forgive you." He was waiting for the man to call back. Each time the phone rang M. guessed it was him. It never was. He began to work on his psychic powers, to see into the phone and pick it up only when he sensed it was the man who called to forgive M. himself. He took to not answering it unless he had some nameless sense it was that man—and then, in a fit of self-doubt, he'd pick it up to check. And when the voice wasn't the man's, even before the person on the line began to speak, M. hung up. M. scratched his back so hard the wooden hand broke off in the matted hair. He stared at the bamboo rod in his hand in disbelief. He reached behind him, down through the neck of his shirt, up through the back of his shirt, but could not reach it. The wooden hand was lodged between his shoulder blades, just out of reach, and couldn't be removed.

M. was a man with a hand caught in the weave of the prayer rug on his back. That is how he thought of himself as he walked to the refrigerator to get another beer. That's how he thought of himself when the phone rang and he sensed that it was the call he'd been waiting for. He picked the phone up on the second ring and hurriedly said, "Hello."

"Don't hang up!" the voice croaked, sounding stricken, deathly.

"Hello?" M. said again, dazed, concerned, not able to put the voice to another human being.

"It's me. Your mother. Don't hang up."

"Mother?"

"I've been calling and you don't answer. I've been worried." His mother's voice grated against him—the monotone growl in which it uttered its concern. It was a voice that in M.'s ear ceased to be human, a mechanical voice whose bass tone was mechanical. "You've thrown my sales off. Did you know that? You're stopping me from earning—"

M. hung up. He didn't feel guilty. He didn't feel exhilarated. The gesture contained no repressed anger at his mother for his upbringing. He wasn't sending her a message. He acted out of an irritation that felt like madness, which seemed to excuse him from simple human obligations: being polite, listening to your mother croak her concerns. It didn't feel freeing; it felt instinctual. M. felt as if he'd become an object or an animal. When the phone rang again, almost immediately, M. picked up and shouted, "Don't call me again!"

"I had thought you'd wanted me to call again."

"I'm sorry," M. stammered, flustered, "I thought you were some-one else."

"Who?"

"My mother." M. felt for the first time a pang of guilt for what he'd done.

"I see," the man said. "You should apologize to your mother."

M. didn't say anything. He just waited. And then, hesitant but inspired, said, "You could forgive me."

"It's not for me to forgive you for that."

M. waited. He felt idiotic, childish. He took a long pull from his beer and sighed.

"I called to say that I've sent you a package, and it should arrive in the mail tomorrow."

"What did you send me? How do you know where I live?" M. spoke with more panic than he actually felt.

"It's easy to know these things."

"Why me?"

"I told you why. I've called to forgive you."

"What's your name?"

"There's no need to know my name. It's enough that I know yours, Moses." And then the man hung up.

. . .

M.'s mother named him after his father whom she would say of after he died, "He's crossed the river," in her musical, riverlike voice. After his father died, M. refused to be called by his father's name who, he thought, crossed to the other side of the river without him. M. couldn't betray his father so he betrayed his father's name. He wouldn't answer to Moses, only to M. What felt to him as a young man a furious response to his father's death, had in his adult life taken on a different significance, and he came to feel in the initial that was his name the broken promise of his father's life. M.'s name was his father's memorial.

No one had called him Moses in over thirty years. The sound of his name in the man's voice uncannily gave M. back to himself, as if being reintroduced to an identical twin whose existence had become only rumor, so long had he been missing. M. felt doubled. His name had lived its own life silent beneath his own. The realization, rather than unsettling him, calmed him. The nervous energy of the last few days, the manic bouts of anger and frustration that plagued M. ever since the man first called, subsided—and M. felt in himself a rolling, abiding calm, a wave cresting widely within a wider wave, a double music breaking on the shore. That shore, M. thought, was this day, was every day—the strand on which the self, or the selves inside the self, broke, and in breaking, became chorus.

M. stopped watching the trials at night. He'd drink a beer on his front steps at night and watch the day grow dimmer. When the phone rang he didn't answer it. Sometimes, as there was no answering machine, the phone would ring dozens of time, the person calling unable to believe that M. no longer would pick up and say "I forgive you." It wasn't that M. had forsaken the idea of forgiveness, he just thought, as he watched the leaves darken at a slightly quicker rate than the sky, that forgiveness worked even when he didn't utter those words. Letting the phone ring was just as good, he thought, maybe even better. The need to be forgiven stops at being forgiven, and maybe the kindest thing he could do was to let the need to seek forgiveness be without end. Or, at least, to not end it himself.

The next day the package arrived in the mail. It had no return address. The man had simply written, in brown ink in looping figures, M.'s own address again. The package was large but not very heavy. M. pulled from it ten objects, almost all the same size, wrapped in yellowed newsprint that, carefully unfolded, contained ads and articles in a language M. could not identify. He put the papers aside, underneath the iron doorstop he kept on the porch, to stop them from blowing away. Then M. placed the objects around him. They were bronze. The largest piece seemed like a case for the discs—each of which fit inside it. The discs were etched with symbols that looked vaguely Hebraic, and they ringed the outermost edge of the disc, each with a flamelike flourish where the figure ended. Circles were etched onto the disc at regular intervals, echoing its own shape, and darker, deeper lines marked trajectories that broke, in their parabolic flight, the strict geometry. Those dark lines clustered in various segments on the different discs, so that the upper hemisphere of one would be thick with lines, and the same area on another would be oddly blank, the bronze, even so aged, maintaining a mirrorlike quality. A circular grid fit on top of the discs, superimposing on the etched lines its own structure: a circle inscribed with words M. could not read, but across which he rubbed his finger. The grid marked off other quadrants on the disc below it, not circular in shape, but segments of circles whose curves swept along the general pattern without ever completing it. Lastly, a piece, in metal of a slightly different quality—not as heavy, not as deep in luster—what seemed to be a spinner, as from a child's game, whose hole in the middle matched up with the holes in the center of the grid and the discs. M. examined each piece and put each back down: a semicircle surrounding him. M. picked up the envelope again and, pulling it open wider, peered in. He saw a folded piece of paper and, pulling it out and unfolding it, found a pin taped to the page, and written on it, in the same handwriting as on the envelope itself, "For you to assemble."

M. carried everything inside and laid the pieces on his kitchen table. The object seemed simple enough to construct. M. put each disc inside the case, placed the grid on top of it, placed the spinner on top of the grid, and put the pin through all of them, inserting the clasp that held the pin in place where it poked through the case's underside. The object felt heavier than M. imagined it would, as if in assembling it, it became more than the sum of its parts. It was a thoughtful weight in his hand. It seemed to him, in the afternoon light coming through the window, that the object was both bright and dull. The etched symbols, the etched lines, looked darker than on the porch, a brilliant blackness, almost onyx in its depth, and the longer M. stared, the more that darkness seemed glinting, darker darks within darkness. M. stared at those etched lines so long, letting his eye follow circuit after circuit across the face of the topmost disc, that when he finally shifted his eye back to the bronze plate itself it seemed to burst into flame in his vision—a sight so convincing M. felt his hand burn and reflexively dropped the disc, which hit the table at an angle, fell to the floor, and lay there, unbroken, a dull ringing in the room from the metal being struck.

The phone rang, and disoriented by the sudden break in his reverie, M. picked it up.

"You built it."

"Yes," M. said, as he stood above the object, gazing down on it. He did not feel like himself, a fact he was about to tell the man on the phone. "I don't feel—"

"Do you know what it is?"

"No."

"Do you know what it's used for?"

"No. I think, maybe, it's for navigation—a kind of map."

"Good. That's true. It's an astrolabe."

M. was silent. The man was silent. He held the phone to his ear and stared at the astrolabe on the linoleum and the silence lasted a long time.

"There once was a man," the man said," who became convinced the sun was a mirror and he lost his mind. His name was Zacuta. He was an old man, and he's older now. He was a rabbi. His ancestors had traveled along the silk routes, and they brought back with them knowledge from the east, which was to them a far greater commodity than spice. They learned astronomy and navigation, and brought back with them to Spain early seafaring tools, including the astrolabe. Zacuta made many improvements on the device so that, once the solar height could be established, a boat's position could be calculated.

This man, this Zacuta, could think of little else but the astrolabe. He devoted his life to its accuracy. He innovated. He thought the discs were the door that opened into a new age, another world. I cannot tell you the nature of his advances, because I don't understand them myself—it is, in ways, a lost knowledge, even though the device is simple. But simplest things hold their mystery with great secrecy. It was to that secrecy Zacuta lent his faith. What for others was a practical device, for Zacuta was a spiritual one. In his time, he became renowned for his astrolabes. The wider his fame grew, the deeper his absorption became in the mystical, as he thought of it, minutia of the tool. Beneath a practical use, navigation, was a mysterious use, navigation of another sort. He became a very rich man, a very famous man. The device changed the world. The conquistadors sailed with them. Cortez carried his in a leather bag he stitched himself from the skin of a lamb from his estate. Magellan discovered the world."

"Yes," M. said, staring down at the astrolabe glowing on the floor, unable to turn his eyes away from it. The prayer rug itched, pulsed, with an intensity he hadn't felt in days. He had nothing to scratch it with. The discomfort didn't distract his attention so much as focus it, and the more focused he became, the more intense his discomfort became until, as the man began to speak again, it verged on pain.

"Zacuta saw too what his work had done. He heard the reports given to royalty of the wondrous savages in the new world, their riches. He heard about their deaths by the thousands. He listened as others spoke of conquest—of how the natives' obsidian-edged weapons, so sharp they could cut off a horse's head with one stroke, shattered against the soldier's armor. He saw the rings on the severed hands the conquistadors brought home as souvenirs. Zacuta heard and saw and thought 'This is what I have done.' Of course, this is my hypothesis. None of this story is written down. It was told me to as I'm telling it to you."

M. listened. He wanted to respond, to ask a question. But he felt transfixed by the astrolabe, by the voice speaking to him, and by the pain on his back, all of which twined together. He couldn't separate his sensations. The voice glowed, the vision burned, the pain listened.

"It was then that something snapped in Zacuta's mind. He closed shop. He made no more astrolabes. He destroyed all save one, inscribed with words and patterns that related to nothing in the known world. The language itself was his invention—an alphabet he claimed to see in the sun when he looked in it. He spent his time reading the sun. He'd look up at it, and quickly look away, close his eyes, and find the words in the sun's phosphorescent afterimage. He claims not to have been able to read them himself. He wrote down what he saw. He could not speak it. And then one day, he looked up and saw no words but instead an image—a man he thought was himself. He stared so long he went blind. His reason broke with his eyes. He died speaking words that to everyone's ears sounded like nonsense."

M. felt nauseous. His knees were shaking. The room felt impossibly bright.

"Moses, do you know how I know this story?"

"No."

"I know this story because I am a Zacuta. I am the next to last of the line. And I'm telling you because you are a Zacuta. After you there are no more. The astrolabe you assembled, that I sent you—it was his. And now it's—"

M. put the phone down. He put it in on the table. He didn't hang it up. He could hear the man still speaking, still telling the story, the story that was also his story. The voice sounded far away, small, higher in pitch, coming out the receiver on the wood.

M. walked to the window. The sun was bright in the upper half; there was no tree in the yard to block it. The light from the sun poured in on M. He looked at it. The pain from the prayer rug hurt so badly it became a prayer itself—a form of attention he could not diminish. He stared in the sun. He couldn't turn his eyes away. The longer he looked the more varied was the sun's light, not yellow, but yellow within which a solar white gleamed, verging into iridescent purple, as on the back of a dove's neck, and suddenly silver, reflective—a mirror in the sky. He could see it. He could see his father's face in the mirror in the sun in the sky. A chime filled his ear. He felt weak. He thought he might collapse, but the chiming continued—up and down the musical scale. He realized it was his doorbell. Someone was pushing it over and over again. He thought at first the sun had been ringing. The phone on the table was silent. Wherever M. looked he saw the image of the sun in his eye, burned there. He thought he might be going blind. His back felt as if it had caught fire. He stumbled through the doorway. The darkness of the living room seemed impenetrable. He knocked over a side table. He heard a water glass break. He felt himself walking through the water. The chiming had stopped. In a voice that seemed inhuman, toneless, guttural, metallic, he heard his name being yelled over and over again: "Moses, Moses, Moses. Open the door. Moses, Moses, Moses. Open the door." A chant he walked toward, stumbled toward.

He wanted something. He didn't know what. He knew the door must be near. He knew he must find the knob and twist the lock. He knew he must find the strength to somehow open it. He kept knocking pictures off the wall. He could hear the glass breaking as the frames broke against the ground. He thought the prayer rug on his back was burning him. The sun had lit him on fire. He had maybe always been on fire. He didn't know. He wanted something. He didn't know what. He found the knob. It was cold in his hand. He unlocked it. The door opened a crack. "Moses, Moses, it's me. I was worried. You haven't been answering the phone." He pushed the door open. He heard his mother's voice. He heard it for the first time, he thought. He heard the riverlike music in it. He thought it's her voice that can put out the flame. He stood in the threshold. He couldn't see his mother but knew she was there. "I'm sorry," he said. And when he said it he fell over; he could no longer stand. He fell forward in the doorway, blocking the entrance with his body, his back filling the doorframe, so that his mother had to step on him, step on his back, on the prayer rug of his back, to go in the house and call the ambulance. And when she found the phone on the table, there was no one on the other line—just a single tone repeating over and over again, that the line was busy, off the hook, or that no one was at home.

Epilogue:
Puzzle and Music Box

My father called to say a gift was on its way. It was for my three-year-old daughter, but I'd be interested in it too. More than interested. This gift, he said, would "blow your mind." It would "knock your socks off." My father loves my daughter past bounds, loves her wildly, adoringly—a love that often find expression in gifts. I've come to anticipate such gifts with a healthy amount of wariness. Each present is heartfelt, undoubtedly, but are often things my wife and I would tend not to purchase ourselves: plaid dresses with white-lace collars that looked as if it might be the uniform to a preschool prep school, teddy bears larger than the child trying to hold it. The last such gift, sent a few months before, for no occasion other than kindness, was a porcelain music box within which a poem, printed in gold-gilt cursive, read: "I was never so blessed / as the day you were born." It was gift meant to be precious. It had all the clues that speak to a child of its value: the milky white material with a heft to it, the brass filigree around its edge, airbrushed flowers on the lid, morning glories, maybe, but pinker, larger—orchids perhaps. The poem begins as a dedication, with a florid FOR emblazoned in gold on the inside cover, and where my daughter's name should next appear (the precious is always personal) was a small piece of paper on which my father had typed my daughter's name, Hana, in italicized Times New Roman. He taped her name in on a scrap of copier paper. Then the golden engraving began again.

When Hana turned the key in the box, the hidden metal cylinder began to spin and out came the song, in the tinny pinpricks of the medium's music, "You Are So Beautiful." When the box is shut the music stops, the poem is hidden. Sometimes I find Hana on her bed with the box open, listening to the music in strange reverie. She loves it; I, of course, have my questions.

. . .

I told Hana that Grandpa had sent a present that should arrive in a few days and she, being at the age where the idea of a "gift" or a "surprise" is the finest thing in the world, began her anticipatory questions. "Is it here, Daddy?" ad infinitum, until the package would actually arrive. Her excitement is contagious enough for me to feel excited; it's an enthusiasm I can't help but stoke with my own repeatedly uttered "Soon, it will be here soon." The best part of waiting for the gift to come is asking Hana what she thinks it might be. "An elephant." "A macaroni bowl without macaroni." Nothing else gives me such a sense of how astonishing desire is. Desire gives equal weight to things of radically different worth. Hana would cycle through the possibilities at every meal. "A teddy bear." "A piece of glass." "Crayons." "A cloud." Desire erases boundaries by easing through them. Desire is wonder in motion. Desire finds that reality's border is loosely guarded. Someone—"reason's viceroy"—is always asleep at his post. My three-year-old girl knows already what many poets would do well to learn: desire pushes through the limit of what is possible, it does not recognize it and retreat.

A cloud in a box would blow my mind, would knock my socks off. I hoped the gift was a cloud in a box. I was curious; I had my doubts.

. . .

My parents divorced when I was three years old—the age my daughter is now. I have very few memories of my parents together, my life before my parents' divorce. My father letting me sip the foam from his beer as I sat on the brown-shag steps that led from the kitchen down to the living room. His yellow car. A small, mean dog named Porsche. I fear I might be making these things up. My mother raised me by herself in Colorado. I had no siblings. I would spend my summers in Ithaca, New York, with my father and my grandparents with whom he lived. My father taught courses like Business Management and Entrepreneurship, things that inspired little wonder in me. What did seem wonderful was spending the summer in the same house my father himself grew up in. We would sleep in the same bedroom, a bed on each side of the room. At the head of my bed the wall was papered in a wilderness scene: the woods at sunset, the color of the sky changing from orange to yellow as the sun set between the trees. There were deer in the woods whose ears were pricked up as if they were listening for a footstep; I would go to sleep thinking I was entering the woods, getting lost in the dark. I liked to pretend, every summer I arrived, that I couldn't remember how the house was put together, which room led to which, and would ask for a "tour." Reassembling the house was reassembling the kid—the kid I was in the summers, so different than who I was with my mother during the school year. The kid who wandered through the woods, who had adventures, who idolized the dad he hardly knew.

Becoming a father myself was an experience that didn't shatter my expectations so much as make me realize I had no expectations to shatter. I didn't know what it was to be a father because I grew up without one. The summers? Those were a different life. The sudden realization of that vacancy in me, that blank resource—that shattered me. Who should I be, who could I be, for this little girl who would need me? It was a question that tormented me in those earliest days when Hana, colicky and crying for hours, could not be comforted through those sleepless summer nights, when my wife and I would wake together to try to calm our baby, when I felt desperate, when I wanted to call someone, anyone, my father, and say, "What's the answer? What should I do?" But there was no answer.

Hana grew out of her colic at three months and began sleeping through the night. This wasn't a feat of parenting but of biology. I was happy, grimly happy, that we all survived. Things got easier—they're still getting easier. But moments still come when the same fear suddenly blurs the outline of my image of myself: this father I am who knows how to be a father. Then the man I picture in my head when I think of myself as my daughter's father disappears, and there is no image at all. Just some emptiness riddled by nameless feeling. And I find in myself the same sense as years ago when I held my bawling infant and asked not, "Who is this child?" but asked instead, "Who am I?"

. . .

Hana and I set the large, thin envelope between us on the floor the day the gift arrived. The envelope was sealed too tightly for Hana to open it, metal clasp and tape, so I tore it open and took out the contents. "What is it?" Hana asked, voice wonder filled, expectant, hopeful.

What I took out was a picture of myself. I'd seen the photo count-less times hanging on the wall of my grandmother's house in Ithaca. I saw it every summer I went to be with my dad—a photo taken from one of the first of those summers. It is, undoubtedly, the best picture ever taken of me. I'm a little boy, maybe five or six. I'm walking on the stone path outside the house that goes past the bougainvillea bushes whose scent seems heavier than the blossoms. I'm not wearing a shirt. I've been in the sun and my shoulders are golden. I'm walking away from the camera and looking back over my shoulder, smiling. My hair is blond. My eyes look only like black smudges beneath my forehead. My mouth, too, is dark where it is open. This photo, more than any other memento of my childhood, defined that time for me. When I think of myself as a child this is the image that comes to mind. For me, it was a photo of the summer happiness that could have been permanent.

"What is it, Daddy?"

"This is a picture of me when I was a little kid."

"Oh." I figured she wouldn't be interested for very long in the photo, but she kept holding it, looking at it, examining it with a min-ute attention I found slightly uncanny. I figured that it must have been strange for her to see me when I was more or less her own age. Then she held the picture out to me and said, "Look, Daddy, Grandpa sent me a puzzle."

. . .

She was right. A thin line coursed throughout the photo, a jigsaw line that cut through the picture. I'd never spent enough time looking at it to notice. I just glanced at the picture behind its frame as I walked down the hall, the image whole in my mind, taking root in my memory, gaining definition there, gaining permanence. Now, holding the picture in my hands, my daughter sitting on the floor beside me, I could see that the image—this image of my own face so many years ago, this image that memory made whole—had cut into it the lines by which it could be taken apart. And that's what we did. I popped it out of its frame, and Hana and I, one by one, pushed the puzzle pieces out from the picture. It had never been disassembled before. A little point of cardboard held each piece to the whole, a little resistance to push through. I tried hard not to think about the process and mostly failed. Sitting on the floor, taking apart my childhood self, this picture of me that looked up at us as we dismantled it, piece by piece, with the daughter I was trying to raise so she couldn't be taken apart so. All the little pieces. We spread them on the floor. We found the circular edge and assembled it: skin tones to skin tones, and the impressionistic background of blurry grass and rocks and flowers. We continued to reassemble the photo. And when I had again a sunlit torso, and my right arm again jutted forward below my face—except I had no face, except my arm didn't yet attach to my shoulder—Hana stood up and left, the puzzle not half done.

I wanted to call her back, I wanted to say, "We're not done." I wanted to say, "You can't leave me like this!" but say it in a tone so she knew I was joking. But I wouldn't be joking. I knew I wouldn't be. So I said nothing at all. I felt like a child myself, sitting on the floor next to the undone puzzle. I felt like a child with a child of his own. Parenthood, for me, is inextricably caught in the paradox of being a father and a child at once—a child with a child, a father with a father. A paradox is another form a puzzle takes, one that desire is powerless to solve. It is a condition and not a game. One just recognizes that puzzle in oneself, as oneself—or, at least, I do. Parenthood, unlike childhood, is a puzzle into which no pieces have yet been cut. I know it can be taken apart but I don't know how to do it myself. And until it's taken apart, how do you know how to put it back together again? It is uncanny, unnerving. It feels almost like fate. In fate, the pieces never seem to fit—and then they do. I have a daughter. Her name is Hana. That's the first amazing, impossible piece.

. . .

I'd like to say when Hana left me and the puzzle incomplete that she returned with the music box in her hands. That's what I desired, that recognition of the moment, these gifts through which, uncomfortably, we recognize who we are. I desired it past reason, but it didn't happen. To hear that tinny music would be a form of kinship, a kind of understanding. But it isn't true. It didn't happen. She came back into the room to ask for something. A glass of water? There I was, still spread across the floor. I was looking for the dark smudges that were my eyes. And there was my daughter, calling my name. Not my name. Calling me Daddy. There was my daughter.

I was in pieces on the floor.

She was a name in a box.

Endnotes

The Hut of Poetry

Kabir, *The Bījak of Kabir,* trans. Linda Hess and Shukdev Singh (San Francisco: North Point Press, 1983), 41, 49, 56, 64.

Mircea Eliade, *Rites and Symbols of Initiation: The Mysteries of Birth and Rebirth,* trans. Willard R. Trask (Woodstock, CT: Spring Publications, 1995), x, 34.

Emily Dickinson, *The Poems of Emily Dickinson,* ed. R. W. Franklin (Cambridge, MA: Belknap Press of Harvard University Press, 1999), 152–153.

Emily Dickinson, *Letters of Emily Dickinson,* ed. Mabel Loomis Todd (Boston: Roberts Brothers, 1894), 315.

Walt Whitman, *Leaves of Grass* (Boston: Small, Maynard & Company, 1904), 34.

John Keats, *Keats: Poems Published in 1820,* ed. M. Robertson (Oxford: Clarendon Press, 1909), 198–199.

THE LAUREL CROWN

Ovid, *The Metamorphoses of Ovid,* trans. Allen Mandelbaum (New York: Harcourt Brace, 1993), 21–24.

Friedrich Hölderlin, *Selected Poems of Friedrich Hölderlin,* trans. Maxine Chernoff and Paul Hoover (Richmond, CA: Omnidawn, 2008), 77.

THE INDWELLER'S AVERSION

Henry David Thoreau, *Walden* (Boston: Ticknor and Fields, 1854), 8, 20, 47–53, 67–68, 80–81, 84, 92, 96, 107, 144, 153, 168–169, 185, 195, 202, 218, 314, 327–329.

Jane Ellen Harrison, *Prolegomena to the Study of Greek Religion* (Cambridge: Cambridge at the University Press, 1903), 6–7, 9, 89–90, 125.

Ralph Waldo Emerson, *Essays: First and Second Series* (Boston: Ticknor and Fields, 1865), 39, 235, 242–243, 330, 350.

Stanley Cavell, *The Senses of Walden* (San Francisco: North Point Press, 1981), 27.

William Carlos Williams, *Selected Poems* (New York: New Directions, 1985), 291.

Caroline Walker Bynum, *Metamorphosis and Identity* (New York: Zone Books, 2005), 39, 75.

THE NIGHTINGALE'S DROUGHT, THE NIGHTINGALE'S DRAUGHT

William Blake, *Songs of Innocence and Experience* (London: W. Blake, 1826).

T. S. Eliot, *The Waste Land: A Facsimile and Transcript of the Original Drafts,* ed. Valerie Eliot (New York: Harcourt Brace, 1971), 136–137, 140–141, 144, 146.

Ralph Waldo Emerson, *Essays: First and Second Series* (Boston: Ticknor and Fields, 1865), 304, 307.

James Frazer, *The Golden Bough* (New York: Penguin, 1996), 13, 77–78, 80–81, 99.

William Wordsworth, "Preface to Lyrical Ballads (1802)" from *Toward the Open Field: Poets on the Art of Poetry 1800–1950,* ed. Melissa Kwasny (Middletown, CT: Wesleyan University Press, 2004), 21.

Anne Carson, *Eros the Bittersweet* (Princeton, NJ: Princeton University Press, 1986), 75.

Samuel Taylor Coleridge, *Biographia Literaria,* ed. J. Shawcross (Oxford: Clarendon Press, 1907), 167.

John Keats, *Keats: Poems Published in 1820,* ed. M. Robertson (Oxford: Clarendon Press, 1909), 107–112.

John Keats, *Letters of John Keats to His Family and Friends,* ed. Sidney Colvin (London: Macmillan and Co., 1891), 184.

TYPHONIC MEDITATION

Plato, *Selected Dialogues of Plato,* trans. Benjamin Jowett (New York: Modern Library, 2001), 118.

ON VERDANT THEMES

Marcel Proust, *In the Shadow of Young Girls in Flower,* trans. James Grieve (New York: Viking Penguin, 2004), 297, 299, 373, 379–380.

MEDITATIONS IN THE HUT

John Bunyan, *The Pilgrim's Progress* (London: Simpkin, Marshall, and Co., 1856), 11.

John Keats, *Letters of John Keats to His Family and Friends,* ed. Sidney Colvin (London: Macmillan and Co., 1891), 256.

Lewis Hyde, *Trickster Makes This World: Mischief, Myth, and Art* (New York: Farrar, Strauss, and Giroux, 1998), 318.

Daniel Heller-Roazen, *Echolalias: On the Forgetting of Language* (New York: Zone Books, 2008), 191–192.

Dan Beachy-Quick is the author of five books of poetry, most recently *Circle's Apprentice* (Tupelo Press, 2011), as well as the collaborative project, *Conversities,* written with poet Srikanth Reddy. *A Whaler's Dictionary,* his collection of meditations on Melville's *Moby-Dick,* appeared from Milkweed Editions in 2008. Beachy-Quick teaches at Colorado State University, and lives in Fort Collins with his wife and two daughters.

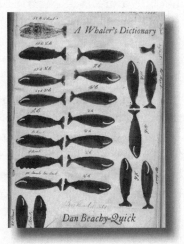

Milkweed Editions

Founded as a nonprofit organization in 1980, Milkweed Editions is an independent publisher. Our mission is to identify, nurture and publish transformative literature, and build an engaged community around it.

Join Us

In addition to revenue generated by the sales of books we publish, Milkweed Editions depends on the generosity of institutions and individuals like you. In an increasingly consolidated and bottom-line-driven publishing world, your support allows us to select and publish books on the basis of their literary quality and transformative potential. Please visit our Web site (www.milkweed.org) or contact us at (800) 520-6455 to learn more.

Milkweed Editions, a nonprofit publisher, gratefully acknowledges sustaining support from Maurice and Sally Blanks; Emilie and Henry Buchwald; the Bush Foundation; the Patrick and Aimee Butler Foundation; Timothy and Tara Clark; Betsy and Edward Cussler; the Dougherty Family Foundation; Julie B. DuBois; John and Joanne Gordon; Ellen Grace; William and Jeanne Grandy; John and Andrea Gulla; the Jerome Foundation; the Lerner Foundation; the Lindquist & Vennum Foundation; Sanders and Tasha Marvin; the McKnight Foundation; Mid-Continent Engineering; the Minnesota State Arts Board, through an appropriation by the Minnesota State Legislature and a grant from the National Endowment for the Arts; Kelly Morrison and John Willoughby; the National Endowment for the Arts; the Navarre Corporation; Ann and Doug Ness; Jörg and Angie Pierach; the RBC Foundation USA; Pete Rainey; Deborah Reynolds; Cheryl Ryland; Schele and Philip Smith; the Target Foundation; the Travelers Foundation; Moira and John Turner; and Edward and Jenny Wahl.

Interior design by Connie Kuhnz
Typeset in Sabon
by BookMobile Design and Publishing Services
Printed on acid-free 100% postconsumer waste paper
by Friesens Corporation

ENVIRONMENTAL BENEFITS STATEMENT

Milkweed Editions saved the following resources by printing the pages of this book on chlorine free paper made with 100% post-consumer waste.

TREES	WATER	ENERGY	SOLID WASTE	GREENHOUSE GASES
17	**7,902**	**7**	**501**	**1,752**
FULLY GROWN	GALLONS	MILLION BTUs	POUNDS	POUNDS

Environmental impact estimates were made using the Environmental Paper Network Paper Calculator. For more information visit www.papercalculator.org.